PACIFIC RAILROAD COMPANY
AND ROCKY MOUNTAIN DIVISIONS

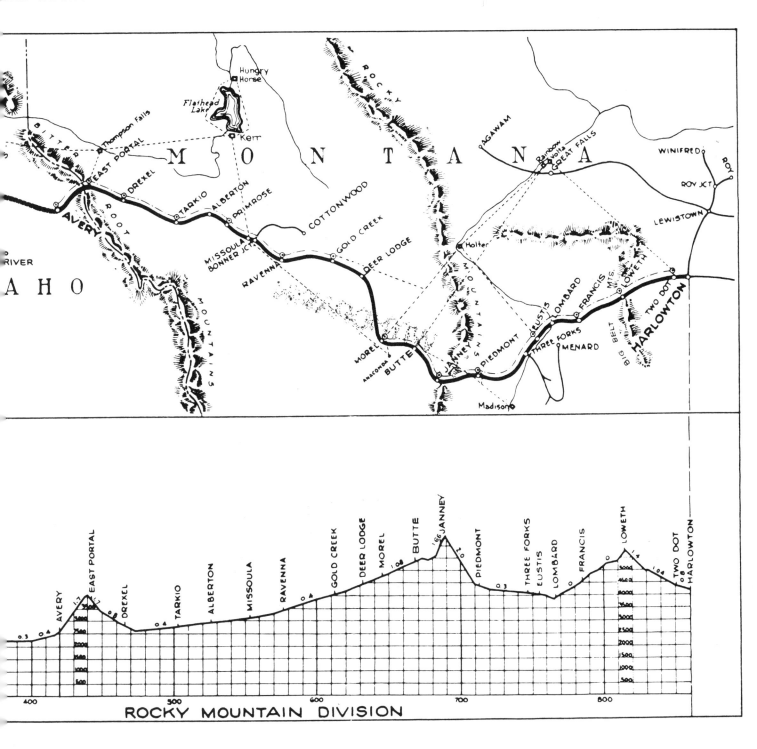

ROCKY MOUNTAIN DIVISION

0-6-0 NO. 1481 SWITCHES A cut of reefers near the CMSTP & P engine house in Spokane, in March, 1951. Steam and smoke, rising from the hard working switcher, obscure Mt. Spokane in the background.

Dr. Philip R. Hastings

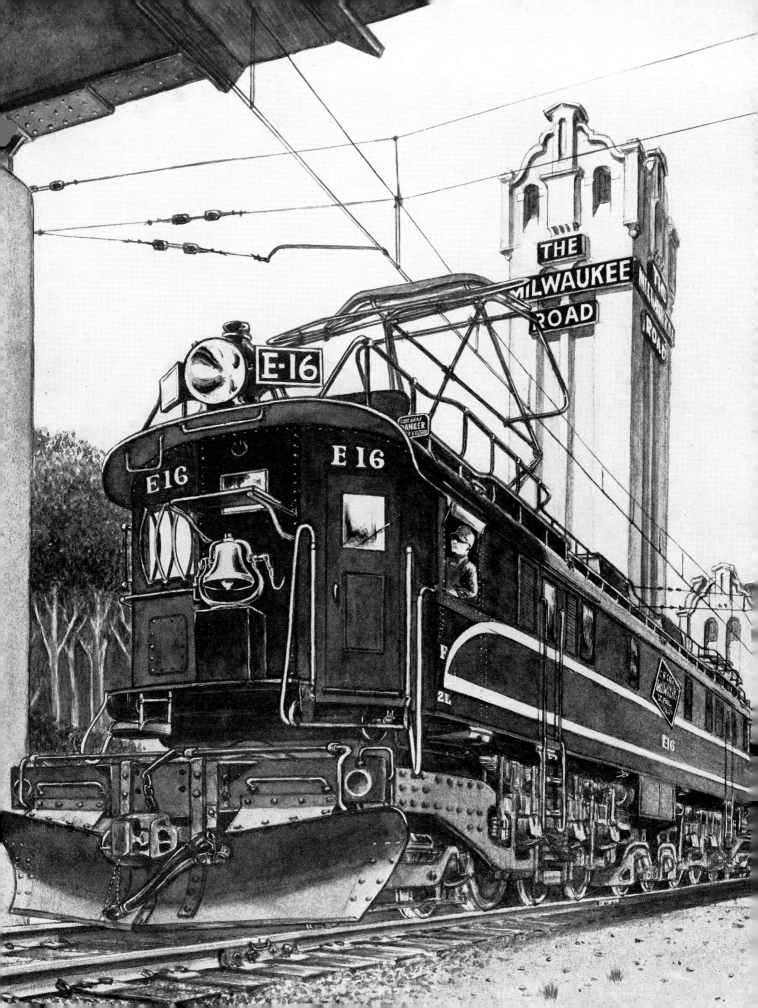

MILWAUKEE ROAD

WEST

BY

CHARLES R. and DOROTHY M. WOOD

Superior PUBLISHING COMPANY

708 SIXTH AVE. NORTH, SEATTLE, WASH.

Printed and Bound in The United States of America

Dedicated

To the officers and employees of the Chicago Milwaukee St. Paul & Pacific — THE MILWAUKEE ROAD.

BI-POLAR E-2 HUSTLES THE Olympian Hiawatha along the single track main through Maple Valley and across the Cedar River in 1957.

Robert E. Oestreich

Acknowledgments

Milwaukee Road West is not the effort of the authors alone, but rather the result of the work of many people. The magnificent artwork was created by railroad artist and craftsman, L.C. Bellows of Salem, Oregon. Stan Townsend, also from Salem, served as the coordinator between the authors and the artist. Wally Swanson loaned his splendid collection of steam photographs, and Don Dietrich contributed both color slides and black and white work. Ed Nolan, student, historian and collector of rare material, made a notable contribution as he searched for material. Philip C. Johnson of Missoula, Montana — photographer extraordinary — did much of the beautiful photography of the electric locomotives. W. R. McGee of Livingston, Montana — longtime friend — searched his collection for photographs covering the railroad. Bob Oestreich of Seattle — Boeing engineer and an artist with a camera in hand — did much of the contemporary work. Don Drew of Pacific Fast Mail, and his friend Dick Harris, searched the Middle West for material. Years ago, Dr. Philip Hastings of Waterloo, Iowa loaned material that is quality work by any standards. Stuart Hertz, W. Wilkinson, Casey Adams, Stan Gray, Jim Scribbins, Jack Anderson, Bob Lindemann, Harold K. Vollrath, Jack Gruber of Potlatch Forests, Inc., L. A. Huffman of Coffrin's Old West Gallery, Wade Hall, Jack Malven, Roger Lins, Tacoma News Tribune, Port of Seattle, Harold J. Davidson, C. C. Tinkham, General Electric Company, Asahel Curtis — pioneer Washington photographer and conservationist, Pringle & Richards Studio, The Seattle Times and Ron Nixon all made notable contributions.

Assistance in locating material was provided by Mrs. Anna M. Ibbotson, Assistant Librarian of the Washington State Historical Society, and by Phoebe Harris, History Department Head, Seattle Public Library, and by the Washington State Library at Olympia.

The contribution made by the people from the Milwaukee Road was invaluable, and Mr. C. E. Crippen, President of the Milwaukee Road, made this assistance possible by giving his consent to the contacting of the officers and other employees of the road in the ever widening search for material. Mr. B. E. Lutterman, Western Vice President, lent encouragement and authority to the work, and Mr. Marc Green, Director of Publicity, served as the contact with the Chicago offices. Mr. Martin Erickson, Public Relations Officer, searched his files for both historical and contemporary material, and was always available for consultation. Ed Notske provided the material and photographs of the Milwaukee Ski Bowl, where he was an instructor for many years. Roy Jorgensen loaned old timetables and pamphlets, and W. Janssen loaned his personal collection of photographs. Mr. Frazier, Chief Electrical Engineer, digging into old records and files, found a treasure in old glass plate negatives, that had been stored away for years and long since forgotten. To all of these people, a thank you and a heartfelt appreciation for their time and efforts.

Charles R. Wood
Dorothy M. Wood

Seattle, Washington 1971

Introduction

In November, 1850, a group of civic dignitaries and railroad officials gathered along a stretch of newly laid track in Milwaukee. A biting cold wind whistled off Lake Michigan as they examined the shiny new locomotive that had been brought two years earlier across the Great Lakes by boat into Milwaukee from the Norris Locomotive Works in Philadelphia, Pa. The little 4-4-0, known as No. 1, was the finest locomotive that could be purchased in the United States or abroad. Coupled to the locomotive, were two open flat cars that were to transport the assembled officials and dignitaries five miles down the track, west to the little town of Wauwatosa. A warning shriek from the locomotive whistle brought the inspection period to an end, people scrambled aboard the cars, and the train, hissing steam and bell ringing, eased into motion in deference to the rather precarious seating in the open flat cars. Once under way, the little engine picked up speed rapidly, to nearly twenty-five miles per hour. As the clear bark of the wood burners exhaust echoed off structures along the right of way, and sparks and cinders sprayed from the stack, the dignitaries clutched their hats and hung on for dear life.

This test run of over a century ago marked two events in history: the coming of the railroad to Wisconsin; and the beginning of one of the major transcontinental rail systems that would stretch from the Great Lakes to Puget Sound, with a network of over 10,000 miles of steel rail in fourteen states, cross five major mountain ranges, and electrify over 600 miles of main line in three states — The Milwaukee Road.

Just two and one half years before the first run of the little American type locomotive to Wauwatosa, in May, 1848, Wisconsin had achieved statehood. The territory enclosed by the new state's boundaries was rich in history. French explorers and missionaries, traveling by canoe and portaging between the lakes and rivers, knew nearly every part of the interior of Wisconsin. Green Bay, visited by Jean Nicolet as early as 1634, and the site of a Jesuit Mission founded by Claude Allouez in 1669, was settled by the French in 1670. Allouez established an earlier mission at La Pointe in 1665. The United States fought with England over Prairie du Chein in the War of 1812, and at the close of the war in 1814, built forts at both Prairie du Chein and Green Bay.

Ruled by the French for over a century from Quebec and Versailles, home of the ancient Mound Builders, hunting ground of the Dakotas, Algonquin, Foxes and Winnebagos, Wisconsin was part of the territory northwest of the Ohio River acquired by the Treaty of 1783, Indiana Territory in 1800, Illinois Territory in 1809, and the Michigan Territory in 1818. The Indian title to Southern Wisconsin was removed by the Treaty of 1833, and in 1836 the Territory of "Wiskonsan," including the states of Minnesota (1858), Wisconsin, Iowa (1846) and part of the Dakotas, was organized. The Territory boasted a population of about 15,000 settlers, trappers and fur traders, but grew by leaps and bounds, passing the 200,000 mark by the time Wisconsin was admitted as a state twelve years later.

The completion of the Erie Canal, between Buffalo and Albany, New York, in the fall of 1825, brought an influx of settlers from the east. The 363 mile long canal, started July 4, 1817, was a remarkable engineering achievement. Through a series of 83 locks, it could raise and lower the canal boats 675 feet over the length of the waterway to compensate for differences in the height of the terrain. An even greater achievement than the locks was the crossing of the many rivers and streams by a series of aquaducts, (one of which was nearly 1,200 feet long over the Mohawk River). In essence the Erie Canal became a true toll water highway that permitted a volume of traffic to flow east and west, reduced shipping costs to ten percent of the former costs, increased land values, and encouraged immigration and settlement of the entire Great Lakes area. A profitable investment for the state of New York, it returned money to the state even before it was completed, and after completion earned several hundred thousand dollars in tolls the first year of full operation. Its success resulted in canals being built or chartered from New England to Delaware. By 1830, over 2,000 miles of canals were in various stages of completion.

In the 1840's, a flood of immigrants came to Wisconsin from another source. Fleeing from unrest in Europe, particularly in Scandinavia and Germany, immigrants thronged to the Middle West and to Wisconsin, bringing their customs and languages with them to create new communities that for years remained as little, and large islands, unique in their new surroundings. Regardless of their background, a problem common to all the residents of Wisconsin, was the problem of transportation.

Table of Contents

SWITCHER E-81 at Deer Lodge.

W. R. McGee

Chapter I
Establishment of the Chicago Milwaukee
& St. Paul

With prospects for growth of the Wisconsin Territory enormous, its transportation facilities remained in the "Dark Ages." Travel over the existing routes was slow, irregular and often hazardous. The first overland routes, the buffalo trails crisscrossing the country, used by the Indians and by the few early settlers, were little better than muddy forest trails, and were clearly inadequate either for heavy immigration or for the flow of commerce. The principle avenues of commerce were the military roads, often unfit for anything other than military traffic, and the great waterway up the Fox River from Lake Michigan at Green Bay and down the Wisconsin River from Portage to Prairie du Chien. Even this route was dependent upon the weather, and while it had served the needs of the fur trade of the early 1800's, (now declining in importance), it failed to meet the needs of the flourishing lead mining industry or the growing agricultural economy.

Early pressure for a railroad came from the lead miners of southwest Wisconsin, seeking a better and more economical outlet to the eastern markets. It cost $1.56 per 100 pounds of lead and shot shipped on the Mississippi and Gulf route to New York, and they argued that with a good road to the Lake and Canal, this could be cut to $.75. Also, moving by way of the Erie Canal, they could receive the money for their sales three months sooner than by way of New Orleans.

On September 17, 1836, the year in which the Territory of "Wiskonsan" was organized, an appointed committee of fifteen citizens from Milwaukee, the Territory's largest settlement, met for the purpose of petitioning the coming session of the legislature to pass an act incorporating a company to construct a railroad from Milwaukee to the Mississippi via Mineral Point.

This charter was not to be granted until 1847. The slow growth of the Territory population during the 1830's (30,945 by 1840), and the panic of 1837 which dried up ready money sources served as a brake on the dreams of building a railroad. Also the belligerence of the Jacksonian Democrats to the railroads created an atmosphere of distrust of eastern capital and fear of monopoly. The farmers were jealous of the city interests, cities within the Territory vied with each other for their own charter, and special interest groups such as stage coach drivers and rural tavern owners, not only bitterly opposed the railroad, but later tore up track when it was laid. Then too, much of the thinking was oriented in favor of plank roads and waterways.

Ambitious men of vision in Milwaukee and environs realized that plank roads, while good for the short distances, would not serve the commerce which could one day be derived from the vast yet unsettled lands west of the Mississippi. One such man, Byron Kilbourn, an engineer, and well educated son of an Ohio congressman, came to the city in 1835 with the vision that Milwaukee could become the most important city in the Midwest, if it could move fast enough to outstrip its rival Chicago by building a railroad to the Mississippi first, and by being the first to establish rail connections with the West and Northwest.

Still the success of the Erie Canal in bringing settlers created the impetus for building more canals,

LUGGAGE STICKERS, courtesy of Dick Harris.

SWITCHER E-82 STANDS IN THE clear at Deer Lodge as the caboose of a westbound Extra
clears the yard throat, August 1971.

Charles R. Wood

with the first thought (agitated for as early as 1829) being to improve the Fox Wisconsin waterway, (for it was via this waterway that the greatest influx of settlers had come), by eliminating the portage at Fort Winnebago with a canal to connect the Fox and Wisconsin Rivers. Out of this proposal grew the desire to improve the entire route from Green Bay to Prairie du Chien with a longer canal between the Milwaukee and Rock Rivers. With some opposition from the Fox Wisconsin advocates, this latter proposal was pushed energetically by Byron Kilbourn and associates. A petition was presented at Belmont, the provisional capital in 1836 for a bill to incorporate the Milwaukee and Rock River Canal Co. This bill was tabled for the session, but a renewed petition presented to the assembly at Burlington in January, 1838, resulted in the incorporation of the company and the approval of the act of incorporation by Governor Henry Dodge. Assuming the presidency of the Canal Company, Byron Kilbourn and the directors petitioned the U.S. Congress for a land grant, and in June, received a grant of 500,000 acres.

Progress in beginning the construction of the canal was slow, and time lessened the need for the project. The large immigration of the 1840's, mostly German, moved primarily to Milwaukee, and then out into the available land opening it to agriculture. Most of this land was away from the avenues of commerce by water, and as the importance of railroads as a means of transportation increased, interest in the canal project declined. With the granting of the charter for the Milwaukee and Waukesha in 1847, the idea for the canal was abandoned, and its directors moved behind the railroad. Secretary at that first meeting in September, 1836, and now Mayor of Milwaukee, Byron Kilbourn was elected the first president of the road at its formal organization May 19, 1849. Changed to the Milwaukee and Mississippi Railroad Company in 1850, it had an amended charter to permit extension of the road to the Mississippi, and an authorized capital of $100,000.

Attempts to transfer the canal land to the railroad had met with heavy opposition and failure, as did the

13

attempts to use the proceeds of the school lands to finance the building of the road. Subscriptions were solicited in money, goods and labor for the grading and beginning of the construction, but cash was needed for the purchase of the rails — $250,000 of it. There was not that much free capital in the entire Territory, and eastern bankers were reluctant to invest in western railroads. The mortgages, on farms along the right of way for stock purchase in the road, also found few buyers outside of the Territory, and eventually the city of Milwaukee issued bonds to meet the cash needs of the road.

Construction proceeded in spite of hostility and many difficulties encountered, and in November, 1850, with five miles of track completed, railroad officials and guests were taken on a trial ride in two open freight cars pulled by Number One (later known as Bob Ellis, Iowa and finally No. 71), a locomotive built in 1848 at the Norris Locomotive Works in Philadelphia and shipped to Milwaukee by lake boat. On Tuesday, February 25, 1851, amidst much fanfare and celebration, the first official trip on the completed twenty mile line to Waukesha was made. A round trip fare was $1.50 including dinner.

The era of railroading had been ushered in. Since the first locomotive had been run in the U.S. in 1825, trackage had increased from a mere 23 miles in 1830, to about 9,012 miles in 1850, and was expanding rapidly. Now the railroad had finally come to Wisconsin with this 20 miles of track and a twice daily schedule (by April) over what had represented a hard day's trip by horse and wagon.

Wisconsin had achieved statehood in 1848, and its population, by 1850, had reached 305,391. Wheat had assumed a dominant position in the economy of the state, and it was imperative to push the rails to the Mississippi as rapidly as possible. In the midst of seeking new financing for this end, the road found its credit assailed due to its failure to pay interest on disputed bonds. These bonds, entrusted to W. P. Flanders, treasurer of the road, in late 1850, to be delivered by him to the company's agent in New York for negotiation, were instead placed, on his own initiative, in the hands of a trio of New Yorkers for a loan of $100,000. This transaction was fraudulent, because these men misrepresented themselves and proceeded to sell the securities to investors. The bonds were finally retrieved by Kilbourn after much difficulty and damaging delay, at a loss to the company of $14,518.44.

The fall out from this fiasco inevitably landed on Kilbourn's shoulders, as well as other doubts concerning his management. A faction led by one of the directors, J. H. Tweedy, challenged his position and seized the books, while those backing Kilbourn had control of the physical properties of the road. Each group had the power to ruin the road, and in the face of this impasse, Kilbourn resigned the presidency in favor of a Vermonter, John Catlin.

Under Catlin's direction, the main line was pushed to Stoughton in 1853, and the first train in was headed by the first locomotive to be built in the state and west of Cleveland. It was completed at the Menomonee foundry in 1853, and named the Menomonee. The company's shop in Milwaukee, under the supervision of John Bailey, was a boon to the company from the very beginning. Rails reached the capital, Madison, in 1854, amidst much rejoicing. There was excitement and celebration where ever the road reached a town, for it brought with it the promise of prosperity, and new towns sprang up along the right of way, sometimes around no more of a nucleus than a station and accommodations for the employees.

In spite of this jubilation and optimism, there were warning rumbles. Politicking and inexperienced engineering did not always result in the most efficient and economical routes. Rising costs, hints of mismanagement, and concealment of financial situations, all contributed to a feeling of unease. The state legislature was busy granting charters to other roads and the competition increased. The country was also heading into the financial panic of 1857, resulting in less available capital and declining revenues to the roads.

In 1856, Catlin resigned the presidency and was replaced by the chief engineer, E. H. Brodhead, extremely popular among the employees. His first priority was to push the completion of the line to

A TRAIN OF THE Milwaukee & Prairie Du Chein Railway Company, successor to the Milwaukee & Mississippi, in this early 1860 photograph, crosses a new drawbridge at Omro, Wisconsin.

The Milwaukee Road

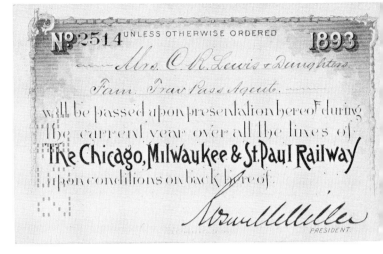

THE TRANSPORTATION PASS issued to the family of Ass't City Ticket Agent, C.R. Lewis in 1893 is signed by President Roswell Miller.

Collection of Edward W. Nolan

Prairie du Chien, so that the line might begin producing revenue. From Madison to Black Earth, Mazomanie and Arena, to Spring Green, Lone Rock, and Boscoble, the rails stretched to Prairie du Chien on April 15, 1857. The line now connected Lake Michigan with the Mississippi River and opened the gateway to Iowa and the west.

Catlin again assumed the presidency in 1858. The financial plight of the company worsened, and in 1860, control passed out of the hands of the stockholders with the foreclosure of the mortgages. On January 18, 1861, the road was offered for sale and reorganized by the purchasers as the Milwaukee & Prairie du Chien Railway Company, with the directors to be New York citizens.

Many other railroads went under during the same period, including the LaCross and Milwaukee, chartered in 1852. Byron Kilbourn, as president of the road became involved in a scandal of such magnitude, that it forced his retirement from the railroad scene. The U. S. had granted land to the state of Wisconsin equal to about ten percent of its territory to be divided between a northeastern and a northwestern railroad. Competition for this land was keen, and Kilbourn, in his zeal on behalf of his road, obtained the grant by purchasing the Governor, most of the legislature and several newspaper editors with railroad bonds. With disclosure to the public, there was a hasty exodus by ex-Governor Bashford for the healthier climate of Arizona, but no prosecution followed, probably because of the difficulty of obtaining proof of individual culpability, as well as the fact that with the withdrawal of the land grant, the Railroad didn't get the land, and with no provision made for the payment of the bonds, the "investors" didn't get the money.

The collapse of the railroads resulted in the impending foreclosure of the farm mortgages, many of which had been sold by the roads to eastern interests at less than face value to raise ready cash. The farmers, once enthusiastic participants in the system, now faced with the loss of their homesteads, arose in anger and protest, charging betrayal and fraud. Their resentment and distrust of the railroads was to have its effect for many years to come, and gave rise to the organization of the Grange. They sought relief through legislative action, which was quickly forthcoming, but in each instance the bills passed were

declared invalid by the state supreme court. The laws did serve the purpose of a delaying action, however, as many holders of the mortgages, rather than face uncertain court actions, came to agreements with the farmers instead of foreclosing. There was also considerable intimidation at foreclosure sales, and even outright sabotage against railroad property — this at a time when the roads were carrying military traffic for the government involved in the Civil War.

To the center of the stage now, came Andrew Mitchell, although he was no newcomer to the scene. He had come to Milwaukee in 1839, a young immigrant from Scotland, to head the Wisconsin branch of a marine and fire insurance company, but the insurance business was only a front for its banking business. It was not called a bank because banks at this time, due to their poor performance records, were distrusted and held in very low esteem. His business acumen and honesty gradually gained public confidence, and his success was such that within fourteen years he had bought out the business. Competitors, and rival bankers from Chicago and Detroit attempted to crush him with raids on his "bank," but his ability to pay off immediately on his certificates of deposit in each case only strengthened his position. He also resisted the repeated attempts of a suspicious legislature to force him into receivership. In 1852, when banking once more became legal in Wisconsin, his business openly became a bank, and Mitchell, Milwaukee's leading banker.

He was also deeply involved with the railroads, both financially, and by serving actively on the various boards. He was one of the original directors of the Milwaukee and Mississippi. His vision was a strong unified rail system to serve the people of Wisconsin, and meet the needs of agriculture, mining and the growing lumber industry, with its control centered in Wisconsin. He now moved in to consolidate the many small lines in financial trouble into one large system. Eventually over 200 corporate entities would go into the Milwaukee Road.

Starting with the Chicago and Milwaukee Railroad, which he served as president, he moved in the direction of both the LaCross and Milwaukee and the Milwaukee and Prairie du Chien. The LaCross and Milwaukee was acquired by purchase, and the western line from Portage to LaCross was incorporated into the newly chartered Milwaukee and St. Paul Railway Company May 5, 1863. Mitchell assumed the presidency and Russell Sage, a New York financier, became vice-president. Sage had been the largest bond holder and the primary owner of the LaCross, as well as holding a third mortgage on the eastern line of the road from Milwaukee to Portage, which was somehow given precedence over the first and second mortgages. This eastern line, the subject of much subsequent litigation, upon foreclosure in 1859, was reorganized as the Milwaukee and Minnesota Railroad Company, and was deeded to the Milwaukee and St. Paul by court decision in March, 1867.

The Milwaukee and Prairie du Chien, in spite of its difficulties, was still the strongest railroad in Wisconsin with many powerful friends, and although it had many communities of interest with the Milwaukee and St. Paul, resisted offers to consolidate the lines or to pool the earnings. The directors also turned down an offer to buy the Milwaukee and St. Paul outright, feeling that somehow they would be the ones absorbed.

Meanwhile, a New York brokerage firm, Henry Stimson & Company, had quietly purchased all shares of common stock of the Milwaukee and Prairie du Chien available in New York. With a short call in November, 1865, they had cornered the market and become the majority stockholders in the road. Upon finding that a clause in the charter of the road prevented common stockholders from voting for the directors, they attempted to change this situation with a bill in the legislature. The Milwaukee and Prairie du Chien countered by threatening to flood the market with new issues of common stock, which would reduce the New York firm to minority stockholders, and the bill was withdrawn. A second bill, slipped in unnoticed, aimed ostensibly at a corrupt petroleum mining company, passed, and turned the control of the road over to the New York group, who promptly sold their stock to the Milwaukee and St. Paul, receiving Milwaukee and St. Paul stock in payment. With this exchange of stock, Mitchell was elected president of both the roads in 1866, and the deposed directors of the Milwaukee and Prairie du Chien threw in the towel, selling their holdings to the Milwaukee and St. Paul in December, 1867.

A LOCAL PASSENGER TRAIN PAUSES to let passengers off at the suburban station of Edgewater, Illinois, about 1900. The living quarters for the station's agent are on the second floor of the station, and laundry hangs on the porch. The unusual lattice work underneath the baggage car, perhaps, was intended to serve as a deterent to hoboes hitching a ride on the truss rods or brake beams.

Edward W. Nolan

With the acquisition of the Milwaukee and Prairie du Chien, the Milwaukee also brought the McGregor Western under its control, because of a prior lease arrangement, an important addition that carried the line from McGregor, Iowa, almost into the Twin Cities. The line was completed under the management of the Milwaukee and St. Paul in late 1867. Mitchell's only real rival now was the Chicago and Northwestern, also consolidating bankrupt lines and expanding rapidly, in Illinois and southern Wisconsin. The relationship, for the time anyway, was somewhat friendly with interlocking directorates and Mitchell serving for a short time in 1869 as president of both lines.

The panic of 1873, provided more lines for consolidation, and the Milwaukee and St. Paul grew rapidly during the 1870's, both by construction and acquisition. A second line into the Twin Cities was opened in 1872 with the acquisition of the St. Paul and Chicago Railway, and in the same year the company completed construction of the line from Milwaukee to Chicago. To reflect the importance of this growing city, the name of the road was formally changed in February, 1874 to The Chicago, Milwaukee and St. Paul Railway Company.

The year 1874 also saw the passage of the Potter Law, the culmination of the efforts over the past decade by the Grange to restrict and control the railroads, by among other things setting rates. The Granger laws and the Grange itself, were a direct outgrowth of the farm mortgage foreclosures, and the feeling of ill will and distrust for the railroads thus generated. Out of the original Patrons of Husbandry, the first permanent Grange had been organized in August, 1868, with a reorganization giving the farmers control in 1873.

The alarmed railroads challenged the Potter Law, but the U. S. Supreme Court, on April 13, 1875, upheld its validity. The agricultural people represented by the Grange, and the primary opponents of the railroads, however, were not strong enough to withstand the powerful support that the railroads could muster. With the unfavorable decision of the courts in regard to the law, the railroads turned to political pressure, both by lobbying and by supporting candidates favorable to the repeal of the law, and to educating the public. The eastern newspapers and capitalists viewed Wisconsin investments with alarm, and local papers became uneasy as all new railroad construction in the state ground to a halt. Finally in 1876, with the election of a Republican governor, and a Republican majority in the legislature, the Vance Bill was passed ending the Granger laws against the roads, and winning the battle against further regulation for some years to come.

THIS POSTCARD MAILED MAY 11, 1900, depicts the depot area at Waubay, South Dakota, forty-six miles from the Minnesota line. Unusual are the two huge water tanks on either side of the station, and the high windmill used to pump water. The writer of the card, a railroad man, tells the recipient to notify his friend in Aberdeen, South Dakota that he has "a squaw picked out for him" if he should ever come to Waubay.

Edward W. Nolan

E-22 LEADS AN EASTBOUND freight into Beverly on the east bank of the Columbia River.
Don Dietrich

In addition to working for the repeal of the Potter Law, Mitchell, seeking to keep the road from eastern control, acquired voter control, and at the stockholders meeting in May, 1875, ousted Sage as vice-president and replaced him with Julius Wadsworth. Now Mitchell and his general manager, Sherborn S. Merrill, continued to work together to produce the "Golden Age" of the Milwaukee Road.

Attention now turned to the problem of spanning the Mississippi River. The John Lawler franchise at the Prairie du Chien — McGregor crossing, never satisfactory to the Milwaukee, had become much too slow for the greatly increased rail and river traffic, and a pontoon bridge was designed and built within the franchise. Taken over by the Milwaukee at Lawler's death in 1891, it was continued in use until October 31, 1961. Further north, an iron bridge was constructed at LaCross in 1876.

By the end of 1876, the road owned five elevators in Milwaukee, capable of storing 3,000,000 bushels of wheat. Its wharfs and grounds were valued at over $2,000,000, and it owned its own sleeping cars — the only railroad to do so. The road also, at this time, abandoned the practice of naming locomotives for people or places, surrendering to the less colorful, but more efficient numbering system.

In 1877, the road was free of floating debt, and had pushed its rails into the valuable timber territory to handle the lumber trade, which had become much too large to be served adequately by river traffic, as Mitchell had predicted years earlier. The following year, hours and wages were improved, helping to foster the "our road" feeling among the employees.

In 1879, the formal acquisition of the Western Union Railroad, gave the Milwaukee access to the Mississippi from Racine to Savanna, Ill. The acquisition of the Chicago & Pacific, in 1880, brought the rail into Savanna from Chicago, with another Mississippi bridge added at Sabula, Iowa. At this time, the Milwaukee had completed 3,775 miles of road, and owned 425 locomotives, 319 passenger cars and over 13,000 freight cars, with the cost of the road estimated at just under $100,000,000. The road now bought grain storage in Chicago, and expanded the yard and depot there. This was also the year that the tilted trade mark was adopted.

Purchases added not only miles of track, but acres of land, and direct land grants were received from the states of Iowa and Minnesota. On September 14, 1881, the Milwaukee Land Company, working closely with and under the same management as the parent company, was organized to buy, sell, lease and improve this land. The land grants, while undeniably of great aid in the construction of the railroads, were a two way street. The Government received many benefits in return. Much of this land was selling for less than a dollar an acre, until the railroads, pushing the frontier ever westward, opened the land to settlers, and provided access to markets.

As the railroad land became more valuable, so did the surrounding salable land still owned by the government, and it reaped the harvest of increased taxes and revenues. It also pulled the country together by providing the government with access to and the means to administer the distant lands which it owned, and to transport the mail. Further the railroads were the means of mass movement of troops and military supplies, carried for the government at reduced rates.

Kansas City, Fargo and Omaha were the aim of the early 1880's, and to this end lines were built across Iowa, Minnesota, the Dakota Territory (through the land of the Sioux), and Missouri (to connect with the Union Pacific and others at the Missouri River), with branch lines extending from the main lines. The brief panic of 1884 slowed things little, and in 1885, 117 miles of rail road was purchased in Minnesota and Dakota in the Red River Valley to protect interests in the Dakota Territory.

Many innovations took place during the 1880's, including scheduling famous "name" trains. In 1887, the Milwaukee became the first railroad to equip its passenger cars with steam heat, and the following year was the first to operate electrically lighted trains west of Chicago. The reign of Mitchell and Merrill, recognized as railroad giants, was coming to a close with the deaths of Merrill in 1884 and Mitchell April 19, 1887. Roswell Miller, who had come to the Milwaukee in 1883 from the Chicago & Western Indiana Railroad, became president in 1888, at the age of 42.

There were changes in the wind for the Milwaukee, which now stretched over five states and the Dakota Territory. The central terminus was gradually shifting to Chicago, and the control of the road was shifting to new interests. Philip D. Armour, a friend of Mitchell's, felt that his packing interests in Chicago were closely allied with the Milwaukee and the use of Gustavus Swift's refrigerator cars, first put on the road in 1874. He bought into the road and became a director in the mid 1880's.

Even more significant was the entrance of William Rockefeller as a director in 1881. He and Henry Flagler were two of the nine trustees of the Standard Oil Trust, whose purpose was to be represented either directly or indirectly with every enterprise which served Standard Oil. This interest was to remain dominant until the Twentieth Century. Rockefeller had not felt compelled to use his position to assert absolute control over the road until certain events nudged him in that direction. Those events were the panic of 1893, the problems arising from the Interstate Commerce Act and the labor troubles of the early 1890's.

In 1886, the U.S. Supreme Court decision that the individual states had no right to regulate interstate commerce or to interfere with traffic across its borders, created a storm of protest from farmers, large shippers and unions, that stimulated congressional action for a federal law. To this end the Interstate Commerce Act was passed to foster competition, to forbid rebates and pools, to forbid higher rates for short hauls than long hauls, to forbid discrimination between persons, places, and commodities, and to require reports and accounts from the railroads. A commission was set up to oversee the enforcement of this act.

The fear of popular sovereignty prompted a meeting of the railroad moguls, called and presided over by J. P. Morgan on January 8, 1889 to "maintain public, reasonable, uniform and stable rates." Morgan maintained that the only alternative to control of the people through government control, was to organize and fix secret rates. The railroad men of the Midwest, still distrustful of eastern banking interests, however, formed their own association.

This evolved into the Western Traffic Association whose aim was to prevent needless reduction in rates brought about by the effects of too much competition. The local rates were also lower because of the short haul rule, and the prohibition against pooling prevented competition on equal terms with railroads more favorably situated. The only result possible under the law, it was argued, was that the strong would absorb the weak, that in the end, too much competition destroys all competition.

The prejudices of people, government and newspapers against "big business" found a convenient "whipping boy" in the railroads and continuous pressure for controls was executed at the state level as well as federal. The "Milk Case" established an important precedent when the U. S. Supreme Court decided against the state of Minnesota, which had given its commission the right to fix rates in certain contingencies without the right of appeal. The Court decision ruled that, while the legislators had authority to regulate and control, the question of reasonable compensation was a judicial one, not to be decided by the legislators.

The labor troubles arose with the soft economy prior to the Panic of 1893. Unionization was taking place with pressure for wage increases, with no corresponding increase in net revenue. In 1893, Eugene V. Debs, an officer of the Brotherhood of Locomotive Firemen, founded the American Railway Union, and in 1894 lent his support to the striking workers of the Pullman Company, which had laid off one third of its workers, and cut the wages of the rest by over thirty percent with no corresponding cuts in rent or the price of goods at the company store. Deb's boycott against the handling of Pullman Cars, resulted in the discharge of those workers, which in turn resulted in a general strike. The involvement of hoodlums and the incidents of violence, prompted President Cleveland, over the Governor's objections, to send in the federal militia. The strike was broken, and Debs and others were jailed.

The Milwaukee, which had not discriminated against union members, and which owned its own sleepers (except for a brief period between 1882 and 1890 when it conveyed a one fourth interest in the cars to the Pullman Company in an agreement by which the Pullman Company handled the cars for them), suffered with the rest. The company was understandably outraged with the rift with its employees, the damage and the loss of revenue. As a result of the strike, the Pullman Company was severely censured by a congressional investigating committee, and it also led to the decision of the U. S. Supreme Court that all the railroad associations were a violation of the Sherman Anti Trust Act. Further it established as immediate goals of the union the right

BUILT IN 1898, the stub end Milwaukee Road station in Minneapolis, with arrival and departure tracks at street level, afforded easy viewing of passenger trains from parallel Washington Avenue. Train watchers were separated from the trains by a long, high iron grill work fence along the sidewalk. The Train shed, several blocks long, could cover nearly the full length of a long passenger train. Arriving trains from St. Paul headed into the station, while the Olympian and Columbian coming from the Pacific Coast, backed in after being turned beyond the station limits.

The Milwaukee Road

THE PACIFIC THAT WASN'T — Engine Number 796, built by the Schenectady Locomotive Works, in 1889, was actually a 4-6-0 type with a two wheeled radial truck placed under the long firebox at the extreme rear of the frames, to take some of the weight off of the drivers in order to meet track loading limitations. When heavier track construction permitted heavier wheel loads, the rear truck was removed, and the locomotive continued in service as originally intended — as a Ten Wheeler.

Collection of H. K. Vollrath

BETWEEN ASSIGNMENTS, A sooty, smoke begrimed veteran of many campaigns, Ten Wheeler 2112, pauses in the yards at St. Paul in June, 1930. Even the large, modern tender cannot disguise the fact that 2112, built by the Rhode Island Locomotive Works in 1887, is rounding out nearly a half century of service.

Collection of H. K. Vollrath

Don Dietrich

to organize, strike, and to bargain collectively.

The Milwaukee was a well unified road, and the harmony among its employees had helped it maintain its independence from outside domination. The trend in the United States towards the control of important industries concentrated in few hands, however, made outside domination inevitable. The Milwaukee was caught in the middle of the battle between the Morgan-Hill interests, and the Standard Oil interests as represented by Harriman, Stillman and Rockefeller, attempting to keep Hill out of Chicago. Hill had attempted at one time to buy the Milwaukee, and acquired control of the Northern Pacific in 1896. Harriman countered by acquiring the Union Pacific in 1897, but was outmaneuvered

by Hill in his purchase of the Chicago, Burlington and Quincy Railroad, which gave him his entrance to Chicago.

During the 1890's, the Milwaukee negotiated a contract with the Union Pacific to use the Union Pacific lines from Council Bluffs, Iowa, including the bridge over the Missouri, to Union Station in South Omaha. All of the infighting showed the Milwaukee, however, that more growth was needed in order to compete with the railroads reaching the Pacific Coast, and thus to share in the more profitable long haul business. The issue soon became whether to extend to the Pacific straight west or northwest.

THE LAST OF THE AMERICANS — Engine Number 98 was built by Rogers Locomotive Works in 1904. Incomplete records do not indicate the disposition of the original tender, but an 0-6-0 switcher tender was used on this fan trip near Chaska, Minnesota in 1950.

Ron Nixon

CHARACTERIZED BY A MONSTROUS headlight that all but overwhelms the front end, motor No. 4 waits at the "St. Paul Road" depot in Racine, Wisconsin, before beginning the trip to Corliss (now Sturtevant) in the early 1900's.

Collection of Don Dietrich

BUILT IN 1854, AND REBUILT in 1871 by the Milwaukee and St. Paul Railway Company, the T.S. Davis, locomotive Number 31 Class H-3, is a classic example of the nineteenth century locomotive builders' art. The fine line striping and painted pastoral scene on the sides of the headlight, the fillagree work and turned brass ornaments, and the polished boiler and varnished cab with striped wheels, with few exceptions, disappeared from locomotives in the early 1900's. Fortunately, when safety appliances were standardized under Federal regulations, the brass ring hand grabs on the cab and tender, and the dangerous footplate steps also disappeared. Many a railroadman lost his arms and legs working on a beautiful little locomotive such as Number 31.

The Milwaukee Road

26

Chapter II
Extension to the Pacific Coast
Moving West

In 1889, Miller resigned the presidency to become chairman of the board of directors. Experienced and competent, he could be trusted to guide and direct the financial policies dealing with the expansion of the road. He was succeeded as president by Wisconsin born Albert J. Earling, who had risen through the ranks. Born in 1849, Earling began his career with the Milwaukee as a telegrapher at the age of seventeen, rising rapidly to positions of train dispatcher, division superintendent, assistant general superintendent, general superintendent, general manager, and vice-president. A Spokesman Review reporter described him in the following terms, "In appearance he conforms to the recognized type of American captains of industry — quiet in manner, ready in conversation, and never halting for a word or an idea. His closely cropped gray mustache fails to conceal his mouth of great firmness, and his keen, gray eyes seem to take in everything, to be held by a retentive memory. He is apparently about 50 years of age."

In the early 1900's, it became apparent to the Milwaukee that it had little choice but to expand to the west coast. The rivalry between Harriman and Hill over the Burlington, and Harriman's attempt to gain control of the Northern Pacific by secret stock purchase, resulted in the formation by Morgan, of the Northern Securities Company, in 1901. This holding company, declared in violation of the Sherman Anti-Trust Act in 1904, by the U. S. Supreme Court, in effect divided the spoils — the western half of the country — between Hill and Harriman interests. For the Milwaukee, lacking fast, direct routes between many of the major cities, to remain independent in an ever constricting network of competition in the Middle West, meant a future of diminishing importance, confined to serving as a bridge and feeder route for the other railroads. To delay pushing to the west coast, would soon place the road in the position of being irrevocably blocked from further expansion and its share of the rich and rapidly growing west coast markets and oriental trade, either by the Hill lines to the north, or by the rapidly expanding Union Pacific to the south controlled by Harriman. The only other alternative was to attempt to work out a permanent agreement with one group or the other for access to the coast, but the board of directors distrusted, and not without reason, allying the Milwaukee with one of the power groups that controlled over 80% of the class I railroads. Without its own outlet to the Pacific, it was at the mercy of its competitors, aware that an agreement today might not be an agreement tomorrow, and would suffer all the inconvenience and uncertainties of arrangements with other lines.

On the positive side, the Milwaukee was a prosperous road, with better than 6,000 miles of track, in sound financial condition, with a total worth of nearly a quarter of a billion dollars, and had an operating income of nearly $18,000,000 with both its common and preferred stock returning 7%. It was an enterprising road, continually consolidating, improving and modernizing. It had the loyalty of its employees, and its management was regarded as one of the best in the country. Further it was felt that the increased revenue from the prosperous territories of the west would pay for the expansion. There had been a tremendous increase in business in the country, due to the increased population and wealth, especially in the plains west of the Mississippi, and manufacturing was growing at a rate even more rapid than that of agriculture. Because the Milwaukee had to rely on the Great Northern or the Northern Pacific to carry its freight and passengers west of Minneapolis, the heavy shipping coming into the west by sea, consigned to points along the Milwaukee, faced long delays in being moved out of the west coast ports, with a resulting tie up of capital, and this loss could be turned into a profit for the road.

There was some concern about the possibility of a canal across the Isthmus of Panama, but international political intrigue, yellow fever, Central American revolutions and seemingly insurmountable engineering obstacles, created doubt that it would ever be built, but if it should be built, it was the belief that it would be used primarily for military traffic, with little economic impact on the transcontinental carriers who would retain the commercial traffic.

There was concern also that Hill and Harriman might unite to stop the road from securing the necessary rights of way and terminals. Surprisingly, both the Great Northern and the Union Pacific stated that they had more business than they could handle, and would welcome the entry of the Milwaukee. In spite of his public statement, Hill, in the past, had not been tolerant of competition in any form and the Great Northern had been planned to take every competitive advantage, with an eye to the prosperity of the new settlers who flooded into the area, and to the Great Northern's share in that prosperity. The Great Northern, alone, had never suffered the financial stresses encountered by other major roads serving the Northwest. In addition, Hill held the mortgage on the strategic Jawbone, over which the Milwaukee must pass.

Within the ranks, William Rockefeller wanted to make the extension a joint venture with the Chicago and Northwestern. This was not at all to Miller's liking. He had long felt the Milwaukee had received less favorable terms in its agreement with the Union Pacific, than had the Chicago and Northwestern, and in line with his desire to maintain the independence of the Milwaukee, pressed for a solo venture. With the withdrawal of Rockefeller's objections the board authorized the Seattle Tacoma extension on November 28, 1905.

BRIDGE OVER THE MISSOURI River, Mobridge, So. Dakota, the heaviest structure thus far built over this great river, circa 1909.

Edward W. Nolan

BEFORE THE COMING OF THE railroad in Montana, overland freight was carried in covered wagons pulled by horse, mule and bull teams. A bull train in Miles City, Montana Territory 1881.

L. A. Huffman

Immediately companies were incorporated in Washington, Idaho, Montana, and the Dakotas in the interest of the Milwaukee, to aid in the construction of the lines in those states, and the cities of the Northwest were bidding for the entry of the road. Construction was started April, 1906, on what was to be a shorter line and over better grades than the competitors. The surveys took longer than the construction, as work was pushed on several divisions at once, rather than one section at a time, as had been done in earlier years. From an engineering standpoint, the road was a remarkable feat, with 2,300 miles of road through the Belts, Rockies, Bitter Roots, Saddles, and Cascades in only three years.

It was an expensive route, however. With no land grants, the road had to buy the land or smaller railroads to gain the right of way. The original estimate, returned by the engineer dispatched by Miller in 1902, to determine the cost of duplicating the Northern Pacific line, was about $45,000,000. Earling upped this estimate to $60,000,000 to be on the safe side, and to allow for unforeseen contingencies. The actual costs exceeded $234,000,000, to be followed shortly by the additional cost of electrification of much of the line in three states, in an attempt to reverse the trend of soaring operating and crew costs on the rugged mountain divisions.

Surveying for the route of the Milwaukee extension actually began early in November, 1905, even before the board of directors had formally authorized construction. President Earling, in an interview in late January, 1906, acknowledged that parties were surveying a route through the Bitter Root country, "but, we haven't heard from them since last winter." Other parties at work around Miles City and Harlowton, located a line that started at Montline, on the North Dakota/Montana border, (about forty miles south of the Northern Pacific main line), and extended three hundred fifty seven miles to a point just west of Harlowton. Beyond this point, the line connected with the Montana Railroad, operating since 1892 through the rugged and beautiful Montana Canyon, to Lombard, on the Missouri River. At Lombard, the line crossed over the Northern Pacific main to the opposite bank of the Missouri, and paralleled the Northern Pacific along the Missouri to Three Forks, where the Gallatin, Madison and Jefferson joined to form the Missouri. West of Three Forks, at Whitehall, the Milwaukee route swung to the south of the Northern Pacific to follow the Jefferson River through Jefferson Canyon (where the Lewis and Clark Caverns were discovered some years later) to Butte, where the Northern Pacific would again be parallel to the Milwaukee.

The Iron Horses All Want to Get Into That Pasture

James J. Hill: I never before saw so much breachy stock in this section!

THESE CARTOONS THAT appeared on the editorial pages of the Spokesman Review of Spokane, Washington in early 1906, depicted Hill's feeling toward the incursion of rival railroads into his "pasture."

The Milwaukee Road

James J. Hill talks welcome, but swings a big club.

The population was very sparse along the Milwaukee route in eastern Montana, in 1906. On the seventy-eight mile stretch between Montline and Terry, where the Milwaukee crossed over the Northern Pacific on the Yellowstone River, there was one ranch house between Montline and Ismay, and one cattle ranch between Ismay and Terry. The bench lands along Corral, Sandstone and Fallon Creeks were unoccupied, and the valley of the Yellowstone,

between Terry and Bluff Port was devoted entirely to grazing. West of Miles City, through the Fort Keogh military reservation, the land was not under cultivation. In the fifty mile distance between Big Porcupine Creek Valley and the first crossing of the Musselshell River, there was one ranch. The country east from Harlowton, for about one hundred miles in the Musselshell Valley was covered with large alfalfa fields for grazing cattle and sheep, with a little wheat and oats grown for winter feed. In the far western part of Montana from Haugan, on the east slope of the Bitter Roots, to Avery, Idaho, the country was largely virgin forest with no trails. The country beyond Avery, almost to the Washington line, was heavily timbered with only a scattering of very small settlements. South of St. Maries, Idaho, a branch line to Elk River and a connection with the Washington Idaho and Montana Railroad (a Weyerhaeuser interest) at Bovill, was surveyed in wild forests.

The public reaction by Hill and also by some of the Union Pacific executive officers to the announcement by the Milwaukee board of directors that the line would build to Seattle, was that this new road would not hurt them as they "had more business at Seattle and Omaha than we can handle." It was true that business was growing rapidly, and the Northern Pacific was handling a train "every twenty minutes" through Stampede tunnel. Still the Northern Pacific and Great Northern took positive steps to see that this business would remain in their hands, polite statements to the contrary. The Portland & Seattle (SP&S) had been incorporated in late 1905 as a joint venture by the Great Northern and Northern Pacific, and construction was started in 1907 below Pasco, Washington on the unoccupied north bank of the Columbia River. The line ran to Vancouver, Washington, just across the Columbia from Portland and the Union Pacific controlled OR & N, neatly removing any possibility that the Milwaukee would attempt to go into Pasco and then build to Portland. At about the same time, Hill tweaked Harriman, who then controlled both the Union Pacific and the Southern Pacific railroads, by organizing the Oregon Trunk Railway to reach into central Oregon from the Portland & Seattle, via the canyon of the Deschutes River that flowed north to the Columbia. The Portland & Seattle line was then extended to Spokane from Pasco almost parallel to the Northern Pacific and bisecting the Milwaukee, giving the Milwaukee one more competitor for the freight rolling out of Spokane to the west. There was considerable activity to gain control of transportation in the entire state of Washington, and block any rival interests coming from any direction.

TRACK LAYING OUTFIT near Miles City, Montana in 1908.

L. A. Huffman

West from Butte, for nearly two hundred miles to St. Regis, the Northern Pacific and Milwaukee main lines would be neighbors along the Clark Fork of the Columbia. At St. Regis, the Northern Pacific main line turned north to follow the Clark Fork, and thereby avoid direct confrontation with the Bitter Roots, while the Northern Pacific branch line continued along the St. Regis River to Wallace, Idaho via Lookout Pass. Northern Pacific surveyors, years before, had regarded these rugged mountains as nearly impossible to cross, except at enormous expense, and had swung the Northern Pacific far to the north around Lake Pend Oreille to avoid the summit, a route that the Milwaukee now chose to build across.

The final location of the line across the Bitter Roots, or for that matter from Butte west, was the subject of much speculation during 1905 and 1906, in The Seattle Times, The Spokesman-Review, and the Seattle Post Intelligencer. In 1905, the Pacific Railroad had been incorporated in Washington with H. R. Williams, the recently resigned general manager of the Milwaukee, as its president. The chief engineer of the new railroad, W. L. Darling, was recently resigned from the Rock Island. Both men had denied any connection with the Milwaukee, but Railway Age Gazette commented on this editorially, wondering why the general manager of the Milwaukee would resign to become the president of a two hundred fifty mile railroad, and be accompanied by an equally prominent chief engineer, unless the Milwaukee and the Pacific Railroad planned to build towards each other. The Seattle papers were not led astray by this obvious connection, and commented favorably on the noncommittal attitude of Mr. Williams, saying this was to be preferred over the grandiose building schemes of some projected railroads that never materialized.

The board of directors of the Milwaukee soon confirmed that construction was authorized, and would begin almost immediately. Upon this announcement, reporters and editorial writers in Spokane and Seattle had a field day, for the projected route between Seattle, Spokane and Butte was far from finalized. The Seattle Times reported that the route would go almost directly west from Butte, then across Lolo Pass, down the Clearwater River to its confluence with the Snake at the western border of Idaho, and "would come very close to, if not into, Lewiston, Idaho," and the "Pacific Road will terminate on the Columbia, at Wallula." This route would have put the Milwaukee across one of the most difficult passes in the West — Lolo, southwest of Missoula, and crossed by Lewis and Clark in 1805 and 1806. The route would have also boxed the road in the steep canyons of the Clearwater and Snake Rivers. The Times correctly predicted, however, that the Milwaukee would reach Spokane via a branch line, rather than by a direct line from Lewiston, that would have lengthened the main line route by two hundred miles. A railroad civil engineer correctly advised The Spokesman-Review of Spokane, that the Milwaukee would never box itself into a river canyon so steep that it couldn't get out with branch and spur lines to reach the wheat fields and small industries, but he also led the paper to speculate that the Milwaukee, after crossing Lolo Pass, would proceed to

31

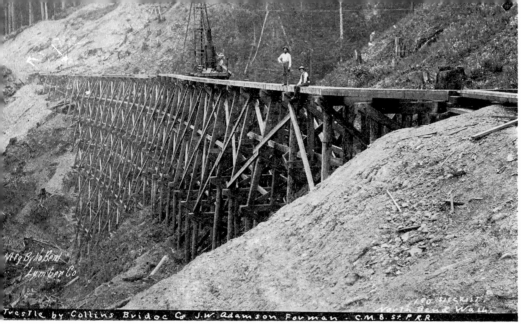

TRESTLE UNDER construction by Collins Bridge Company in Snoqualmie Pass in 1908.

Edward W. Nolan

the Columbia River near Pasco to meet the Pacific Railroad. No one had guessed the actual route following the banks of the Clark Fork and St. Regis Rivers, across from the Northern Pacific, almost to Lookout Pass, and then turning almost due south over St. Paul Pass (originally St. Regis Pass), following the St. Joe River to Avery and St. Maries, Idaho, a remarkable and costly engineering feat. From St. Maries, the line was located around the southern end of Lake Couer d'Alene, and entered Washington some thirty miles south of Spokane. With trackage rights part of the way over the Union Pacific (OR&N), a branch line left the main at Plummer Junction to enter Spokane, and rejoined the main at Marengo, Washington. Thus the main line did not touch either Lewiston or Spokane directly. From Marengo, the main continued west through rich wheat country, far from Wallula and Pasco, to cross the Columbia over

HULL CREEK TRESTLE, MORE spectacular than Change Creek trestle, is built on a sharp curve that approaches 10 degrees and abruptly reverses itself as it coils around the mountains. In this 1911 scene, a westbound freight winds down the mountain, and the cars heel to the super elevation, first one way and then the other.

Edward W. Nolan

a huge bridge at Beverly, in the central Washington desert, a country of wind, sand, rock, sagebrush, rattlesnakes, and jack rabbits.

Across the Columbia the survey continued up the steep pitch of the bleak Saddle Mountains, swinging and spiraling down into the beautiful and rich Kittitas Valley and Ellensburg, to meet once again, the Northern Pacific, on its way to the coast via Pasco and the Yakima Valley. The low brown mountains gave way to forested slopes and ever steeper canyons as the coast bound roads followed the Yakima River through the Ellensburg Canyon and began the climb for the Cascade passes, that drop swiftly, sharply down 2% grades to the coastal plains and waterways of Puget Sound.

The Northern Pacific, in the 1880's, bypassed Snoqualmie Pass in favor of Stampede Pass, slightly to the south, largely because of the report by Captain George B. McClelland of the Corps of Army Engineers. Cautious by nature, McClelland had explored much of Snoqualmie Pass in September, 1853, in search of a favorable route to the Pacific Coast, and concluded that the pass would be too difficult to use in the winter and spring, because of extremely heavy snowfall on the west side. His Indian guides, hoping to adversely influence his report on

CHANGE CREEK TRESTLE RESOUNDS to the tramp of a double headed passenger train working its way up Snoqualmie Pass in 1912. The trestle is listed as bridge number 1 going up the pass, and while not as spectacular as some, it is the first of a series of high and curving trestles that have been in daily use for nearly sixty years.
Edward W. Nolan

1911 IN Miles City, Montana.
Edward W. Nolan

SOME OF THE LARGEST lumber mills in the United States were built in Washington, regarded for decades as the lumbering capital of the world with its seemingly inexhaustible forests of fir, pine and spruce. This modern lumber mill of 1910 was erected at the now largely deserted town of Selleck, on the west slope of the Cascades, and served by both the Milwaukee and the Northern Pacific.

Edward W. Nolan

the pass, had reported that the fall reached twenty-five to thirty feet on the coast side. A more thorough exploration of the route by Lt. Tinkham, in January, 1854 acting on the orders of Governor Stevens of Washington Territory, resulted in a more favorable report. While encountering several feet of snow in the pass, Tinkham did not regard the snow conditions as making the pass unsuitable for a railroad. Nevertheless, the Northern Pacific, to avoid the high cost of heavy construction through the pass located the original line by way of the Columbia and through Portland, Oregon, and later built a more direct route to Seattle/Tacoma from Pasco, following the Yakima River from its confluence with the Columbia into the Cascade Mountains. Lt. Tinkham's more complete and optimistic report was justified by the surveyors for the Pacific Road, and there was little question that the Milwaukee would use this route, then follow the Cedar River down through its watershed into Maple Valley, and by trackage rights enter Seattle over the line of the Pacific Coast Railway.

After the completion of the initial survey along the length of the Pacific extension, the next task was to invite bids from general contractors, experienced in railroad or similar heavy construction. The extension was divided into three general areas for construction: Mobridge to Butte, Butte to Avery, and Avery to Seattle/Tacoma. The McIntosh Brothers of Milwaukee were selected as the contractors for the longest division from Mobridge to Butte, a distance of seven hundred eighteen miles. The Winton Brothers were contracted from Butte to Avery, and H. C. Henry of Seattle for the Avery to Seattle/Tacoma division. Milwaukee personnel handled the supervising and coordinating of the contractors, and the Milwaukee's own building gangs constructed the bridge over the Missouri in South Dakota, and three

bridges across the Yellowstone — near Terry, Montana, at Tusler Crossing, and about five miles west of Miles City.

Each general division was broken down into subdivisions, and construction of the entire line was carried out from many points simultaneously, from Morbridge to Tacoma. The McIntosh brothers, called for bids from sub-contractors for construction on sections of the line along the entire seven hundred eighteen mile stretch. In some construction areas that paralleled the Northern Pacific or where roads were easily accessible, as along the Butte Whitehall highway in Montana, material could be delivered almost to the site, and the work could proceed rapidly. In other areas such as the sparsely populated South Dakota of the early 1900's, construction was hampered by the lack of roads. A new heavy duty road had to be graded along the entire two hundred mile stretch between the Missouri and Yellowstone Rivers to carry material and supplies.

A rain or thaw turned the rich prairie into a quagmire of mud and gumbo, that made movement impossible until the ground dried out again. Severe winter months, with the temperature often falling well below zero, made handling steel with bare hands impossible. Blizzards out of the northwest hampered construction, blending the sky and ground into a moving wall of white snow. A man could lose his way only a few dozen yards from the railhead, as surely as a ship can be lost in a heavy fog.

In 1906, Milwaukee crews were constructing the longest and heaviest bridge yet put across the Missouri. Over a year in the building, it cost the railroad $2,000,000, and not including the long approaches on the east and west, was a quarter of a mile long. The three main spans, of through truss design, towered one hundred twenty feet above the river, with

THIS PHOTOGRAPH OF BELT CREEK trestle and tunnel in Montana, under construction in 1913, dramatically illustrates the reason for the high cost per mile of railroad construction in the West. The heavy equipment, large labor forces, dynamite and muscle power necessary to construct the series of bridges, tunnels, cuts and fills, raised the cost of just one mile above the cost of many miles of railroad built across the prairies.
The Milwaukee Road

IN THE LOWER PHOTO, Porter built saddle tanker 39 takes water from a creek in 1912, and upper, works with a steam shovel and little dump cars near Lewistown, Montana.
W. R. McGee

the rails themselves fifty-five feet above the mean water level. The crossing, aptly named Mobridge, was a few miles north of the former terminal on the Missouri at Evarts. Evarts was bypassed in favor of the more direct crossing beyond Glenham, and upon completion of the main line in 1909, the line between Glenham and Evarts was abandoned. West of Mobridge, the line crossed Standing Rock Indian Reservation, home of the Sioux Indians, and, until 1880, a vast wild buffalo range. Chief Sitting Bull had lived here, and was buried at Fort Yates, not far from the new line of the Milwaukee. The road moved northwest across the prairie into North Dakota, skirting the Bad Lands between McIntosh and Marmarth — an area of curious cones and fortress like hills of sun baked clay and rock.

The three large bridges constructed between Terry and Forsyth, across the swift Yellowstone River in Montana, averaged 1,100 feet in length. The greatest difficulty arose in the twenty-five mile stretch of railroad between the first and second crossing, on the north bank, opposite the line of the Northern Pacific. With no access to this side of the river, it was necessary to ferry supplies in small boats across the river from spurs laid by the Northern Pacific to serve the construction site, and some heavier, bulkier equipment was winched across the river bottom by cable. Rising in the high Rocky Mountains of Yellowstone National Park, and named for the yellow rock formations found in the Grand Canyon of the Yellowstone, the river carried off in its spring flood, a large share of the melting snow pack in the mountains. This annual run-off in late spring and early summer, made it necessary to protect many of the banks and bluffs along the river with thousands of yards of rock riprap, to prevent washing out of the railroad fill. Construction was also handicapped by the large number of streams to be crossed. From Marmarth, North Dakota to Forsyth, Montana no less than two dozen large streams had to be bridged.

At Forsyth, the Milwaukee, after paralleling the Northern Pacific for about eighty-four miles, turned away to the northwest to pick up the Musselshell River at Melstone. This country, like the Dakota section, was unpopulated, and all supplies had to be hauled from Forsyth. Even water was scarce. After reaching the Musselshell, water was no problem, and the trees along the river supplied fuel, but the river had to be bridged at twelve locations, for a better alignment. Where the river channel was straightened and riprapped to save bridging, the irrigation systems of the ranches of the valley were disrupted, and lengthy negotiations and considerable expense were encountered in settling the damage claims. From Melstone to Harlowton, a distance of one hundred four miles, the grade along the river gradually ascended, and the railroad headed almost due west through rolling hills into central Montana.

From Harlowton to Seattle/Tacoma, the Milwaukee would be confronted by five major mountain ranges. The first of the ranges to be conquered, the Big Belt, already had a railroad built across it, through Sixteen Mile Canyon and on to Lombard on the Missouri River for an interchange with the Northern Pacific. That railroad was the Montana Railroad, known locally as the "Jawbone Railroad." The importance of the Montana Railroad to the Milwaukee was — to say the least — considerable. In the first place it occupied the only low pass between the Cas-

A PILE DRIVER works on a wooden trestle on the main line near Vananda, Montana in 1914. Ten Wheeler 2703 serves as power to the outfit.
W. R. McGee

tle and Crazy Mountains, the lesser ranges of the Little Belt and Big Belt. Secondly, the Montana Railroad had completed its line into Lewiston and the rich farming country of the Judith Gap. It also held the key to the possibility of an extension to Great Falls, Montana's largest city, and to the rich grain producing areas north and east of Lewiston.

Richard A. Harlow, a lawyer and real estate promoter from Helena, had organized the Montana Midland (predecessor of the Montana Railroad) in 1893, to bring out low grade ore from the Cumberland mine in the Castle Mountains and transport it to the Northern Pacific at Lombard. The Northern Pacific did not feel that the low grade ore justified extending its line from Lombard into the Castle Mountains via Sixteen Mile Canyon, so the people of Helena had offered a bonus of $200,000 to anyone who would build the road demanded by the miners. Coke and ore concentrate were hauled with considerable labor and expense between Livingston and the mine by wagon teams.

Harlow started the road and managed to get down two miles of track when the panic of 1893 hit. The silver market collapsed, and with it the railroad. With the railroad in deep financial difficulty, Harlow became famous for his persuasive talking known as "jawboning," when he continually stalled his employees concerning their pay, telling them that they wouldn't have anyplace to spend it anyway. He reorganized the road as the Montana Railroad in 1895, secured new capital in the east and began again. The road was completed in 1900 between Lombard and the stage stop at Merino. Harlow had named Lombard for his chief engineer, Arthur B. Lombard, a respected, capable engineer and prominent railroad builder. Lombard returned the compliment by renaming Merino, Harlowton. In 1903, the Montana Railroad was extended north into Lewiston and the Judith Gap area. The judgement of the Northern Pacific, that the hauling of low grade ore from the mines at Cumberland would not pay, proved correct, and the railroad with nearly $3,000,000 invested in it, was in serious financial difficulties. James J. Hill of the Great Northern held a mortgage on the prop-

TEN WHEELER 2505, SERVING AS power to a construction crane, stands on the bridge over Red Coulee during the building of the line to Great Falls, Montana in September, 1913. The long boom on the crane permits it to reach out over the end of the bridge, while keeping the weight concentrated on the completed portion of the bridge.
The Milwaukee Road

ALTHOUGH THE MAIN line of the railroad was opened for through freight service in July, 1909, many parts of the road were still incomplete or operating over temporary trackage. Construction gangs continued to labor on permanent bridges and widened cuts, and spiked down heavy steel, in some areas, until late in 1913.

One way to keep construction gangs on the railroad — which wasn't always easy — was through the serving of good food in unlimited quantities. A good cook and his helpers were key employees on the railroad, and could do as much to keep men on the job as the paymaster. Steaks, an all time favorite, were on the menu daily, along with chicken, ham, pork, platters of fried eggs, hotcakes, hot cereal, fried potatoes, homemade bread, pies and cakes, and fresh strong coffee by the gallon. At dinner the kerosene lamps cast their mellow light on the rough pine plank walls, and on the crude tables filled to capacity. After dinner the smell of pipe tobacco and the drone of conversation filled the air.

The Milwaukee Road

erty, and Harlow sat tight for three years, hoping to extend his railroad to Forsyth and eventually to St. Paul. If his dreams had come true this would have been one of the very few railroads built from west to east.

The Milwaukee had had their corporate eye on this property for a long time, recognizing its strategic position and the importance of the Montana Railroad to the Milwaukee's plans to go to the Pacific Coast. With the Great Northern occupying the "high line" to the north, and the Northern Pacific commanding the Yellowstone route to the south, the only way for the Milwaukee to go west was via the Montana Railroad. The Milwaukee worked out an arrangement to lease the property, and then have Harlow pay off the Hill mortgage, and sell the Montana Railroad to the Chicago, Milwaukee & Puget Sound Railway of Washington, who then deeded it to the Milwaukee in 1910. Harlow realized his dream of extending his railroad to St. Paul by becoming a vice-president of the Milwaukee. Eventually, after paying off the debts incurred when the Montana Railroad was built, he retired to Virginia.

The roadbed of the Montana Railroad had been built as economically as possible, and most of the entire Sixteen Mile Canyon route had to be rebuilt to the heavy duty standards by the Milwaukee. Some of the original roadbed had been built on top of pilings driven into the creek bed, and this had to be kept in operation as the Milwaukee crews blasted rock to straighten and widen the route, which in some places was only one hundred feet wide. The line between Harlowton and Ringling, at the east entrance to the canyon, was also rebuilt. Curves were eased, heavy rail was laid, and much of the original track which was laid right on the prairie sod without benefit of a base or fill, was built up for stability and faster operation. From Harlowton, the long climb up the Big Belt Mountains (forty-six miles of 2% grade), involved curves as tight as ten degrees, and the sumit at Loweth reached an elevation of 5,788 feet.

The Milwaukee crossed over the Northern Pacific at Lombard, and swung over to the opposite bank of the Missouri River towards Three Forks, Piedmont, Jefferson Canyon and Butte. Swinging into Jefferson Canyon, the road began the climb to the summit of the Continental Divide at Donald, and the east entrance to 2,290 feet long Pipestone Pass tunnel. Twenty-one miles of 2% ascending grade, and numerous curves right on the edge of the Rocky Mountains, made the line appear steeper than it really was.

The road descended a 1% grade through the tunnel and a 1.66% grade for ten miles into Butte. From Colorado Junction, one and one half miles west of Butte, the Milwaukee used the tracks of the Butte Ananconda & Pacific to Cliff Junction, until its own tracks, started in 1912, through the very narrow

A WORK TRAIN IS SPOTTED on a siding along the main line outside of Three Forks in 1912. The sign hung on the side of the second outfit car reading "VC Co. CAMP 1912" probably indicates one of the private contractors who helped to build the road.

The Milwaukee Road

LAKE KEECHELUS, WASHINGTON, just east of the summit of the Cascades, is the site of the largest and longest snowsheds on the railroad. The station, agents quarters and order board are long since gone, but in the days before the advent of Interstate 90, the station was a busy place, as the rudimentary highway across Snoqualmie Pass was dangerous and slow.

Edward W. Nolan

CLASS N MALLET helper in pusher service in the Cascades in March, 1912.

Edward W. Nolan

THE EASTBOUND COLUMBIAN TRAIN 18 has just pulled into the Avery, Idaho yard in 1947, behind a Northern type steam engine. The steam engine will be released and an electric will couple on for the long climb through the Bitter Roots, mountains so steep, with rivers so swift and full of rapids, that this country was avoided by the Lewis and Clark Expedition as being nearly impassable.

The Milwaukee Road

THE SMALL SON OF A railroad employee, perched on the steam chest of 0-6-0 switcher, poses with his friends at Avery, Idaho in 1914, a town that the writer of this card described as "a horrible place." The town of Avery was endangered in the terrible Idaho forest fire of 1910 that roared through many counties of northern Idaho and northwestern Montana, destroying thousands of acres of valuable timber. The Milwaukee operated through Mineral County in Montana, and Shoshone and Benewah Counties in Idaho, and the work performed by the employees did much to prevent a greater loss of life. Two trainloads of residents were evacuated from Avery to Tekoa, Washington, and the roundhouse foreman, with the aid of his Japanese employees, set a backfire on both sides of the St. Joe River that saved the town.

Edward W. Nolan

THE HOTEL IDAHO AT AVERY, (the only hotel) has long been a stopping place for Milwaukee crews coming west from Alberton and east from Othello.

Martin Erickson
The Milwaukee Road

Silver Bow Canyon were completed in October, 1913. Except for some heavy rock work in the Pipestone Pass tunnel, work on the Lombard to Butte stretch progressed rapidly, with crews working at many points along the line at the same time from Butte east, and west from Lombard. This faster piecemeal type of construction was practical where access could be provided to the construction site. A decade or two earlier the Northern Pacific and the Great Northern had had to build largely from one advancing railhead, completing bridges and tunnels before the track laying gangs could move on.

The construction on the second division continued on west from Butte, with work also underway at Haugan on the approaches to St. Paul Pass on the Washington/Idaho border, and at Huson, Montana. Again, sub-contractors were at work on many sections of the road at the same time. Coming out of Butte, the Milwaukee, once again paralleled the Northern Pacific. Out of approximately seven hundred fifty miles of main line in Montana, three hundred miles of line were close by or parallel to the

POTLATCH LUMBER COMPANY mill and community of Potlatch, Idaho in the fall of 1913. This lumber company was the one that had the WI & M built. The Potlatch Lumber Company merged in 1931 with two others to form Potlatch Forests, Inc.

Potlatch Forests, Inc.

WASHINGTON, IDAHO & MONTANA Ry. Co. passenger train photographed shortly after completion of the road in 1908 between Palouse, Washington and Purdue, Idaho, for a total of 49 miles of track. In 1910 the rails of the Milwaukee Road connected with the WI & M at Bovill when the Elk River branch from St. Maries, Idaho was completed.

Potlatch Forests, Inc.

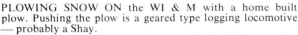

PLOWING SNOW ON the WI & M with a home built plow. Pushing the plow is a geared type logging locomotive — probably a Shay.

Potlatch Forests, Inc.

Northern Pacific. In this regard, the Milwaukee had little choice, as the Northern Pacific following the Missouri, Yellowstone and Clark Fork, had occupied the only really practical rail route connecting Livingston, Billings, Butte, Missoula and Helena.

From Haugan to the east side of St. Paul Pass in the Bitter Roots, the Milwaukee followed the St. Regis River. Curves were numerous, with some as sharp as ten degrees, and there was a climb up a 1.7% grade for fifteen miles before the summit was reached. The tunnel at St. Paul Pass, 8,771 feet long, was the most difficult of all the tunnels to build on the original main line. For six months the bore was pushed through at an average rate of twenty feet per day. The twenty-two mile stretch of main line from St. Paul Pass west to Avery, was the most costly piece of track on the road due to the bridges, fills and tunnels. On the "East Fork Loop" the track runs over a long deep fill, then through a tunnel, over another fill, through a curving tunnel and out on to a bridge, describing a complete semi-circle on the mountain side. In the twenty-five miles between the summit and the water level at the St. Joe, there was a total of fourteen tunnels and twenty-six bridges.

H. C. Henry, the general contractor for the third division, subcontracted with Jacobsen & Lindstrom, J. H. Flick Construction Company, Lorimer and Gallagher, Henry & McFee and C. J. Johnson. Work commenced east and west between Avery, Idaho and Lind, Washington, southwest of Spokane. Passengers to Spokane transferred to the Northern Pacific at Rosalia, Washington, until the joint passenger line was completed into Spokane via Plummer Junction and Marengo, in 1914. From Lind, work progressed westward, through the Saddle Mountains and across the Columbia at Beverly over a mile long bridge. At the Northern Pacific crossing at Murdock, just west of Ellensburg, an extensive material yard was built, and tracks pushed east towards the Columbia in February, 1908.

In July of the same year, with the heavy snow pack in the Cascades largely gone and streams past the flood stage, track was laid to Ragner, four miles from Cedar Falls on the west slope of the Cascades. A temporary "high line" was constructed crossing Snoqualmie Pass at an elevation of 3,010 feet. The line involved 1,239 degrees of curvature and a climb of an additional 446 feet, resulting in a grade of

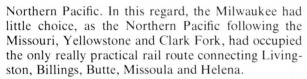

ROD LOCOMOTIVE No. 23 on the WI & M bringing a train load of logs to the mill at Potlatch. The forests around Potlatch contained some of the finest stands of White Pine to be found anywhere in the United States. One record train load of one hundred and four cars (41' flats) carried 1,100,000 board feet!

Potlatch Forests, Inc.

THE COVERED BRIDGE OVER THE Skykomish River, on the Cedar Falls-Everett branch near Monroe, was one of several built by the Milwaukee Road in Washington, in the early 1900's. The weathered wooden cover, which had not felt a coat of paint in decades, was designed to protect the primary structure from the elements, but was a fire hazard even in this day of diesels, and has been removed.

Stuart Hertz

MONROE, WASHINGTON IN 1908 — here the Cedar Falls Branch, after crossing the covered bridge over the Snohomish River, picks up the rails of the Great Northern, and by trackage rights continues on into Everett, Washington.

Edward W. Nolan

AN SD-9 EMERGES INTO SUNLIGHT from the covered bridge across the Skykomish River. Following are two SD-7's, still hidden from view inside the bridge. After crossing the bridge the line swings sharply left to merge with the tracks at Monroe. The Milwaukee gains entry into Everett, thirty miles north of Seattle, by virtue of running rights over the Great Northern main line.

Stuart B. Hertz

2.75% on the west side. Even so, it offered a much better grade than the original Northern Pacific line over Stampede Pass, without the complications of switchbacks. Upon completion of the Snoqualmie Pass tunnel (11,890 feet long) in 1915, the "high line" was abandoned. Three and one half miles longer than the tunnel route, much of the grade was later used as a part of State Highway number 10, and the station at the summit, Laconia, was rebuilt into a lodge and restaurant. The station was replaced by facilities, just east of the tunnel at Hyak — from the Chinook word Hyack, meaning big hole.

Five miles east of Hyak, the railroad skirts the south shore of Lake Keechelus, one of the largest lakes in the Cascades. Steep, rocky cliffs rise from the shore of the lake, and huge snowsheds were built to protect the road from snowslides and avalanches that come thundering down especially during warming periods in the winter. Then the very wet heavy snow, no longer able to maintain its precarious hold

on the bare cliffs, will slide off, burying everything in a fast moving wall of snow. Keechelus is an Indian name meaning white stallion, and there is an Indian legend that the lake is possessed of the spirit of a gigantic white stallion that lures bands of horses to their death in the lake. The Indians would not camp near the lake or use the grazing land along the banks.

Chief engineers played a little game of musical chairs when W. L. Darling, the first chief engineer of the Pacific Railroad Company which was incorporated in October, 1905, and became the Chicago Milwaukee & St. Paul Railway Company of Washington in January, 1906, resigned to become chief engineer of the Northern Pacific, replacing E. J. Pearson, chief engineer of the Northern Pacific, who resigned his post to become chief engineer of the Chicago, Milwaukee & St. Paul Railway of Washington.

The branch line from Cedar Falls to Monroe, built in 1911, followed very closely Lt. Tinkham's ascent

44

of the west side of the Cascades from Everett, following the Snohomish and Snoqualmie Rivers.

Tacoma was the planned western terminus for a variety of reasons, all of which were important to the Milwaukee, if it ever hoped to pay for the extension of the line. Perhaps, most important, was the location of Tacoma, in the heart of the western Washington lumbering area, from which the Milwaukee planned to derive its greatest single source of traffic. Known as the "Lumber Capital of America," Tacoma had 10,000 men employed in its sawmills, which were cutting 25% of the timber crop in the Pacific Northwest. The lumber production alone would account for thousands of car loads annually. Also important, was the steadily growing trade with the Orient, and Tacoma offered one of the best harbors on the entire Pacific Coast. The Great Northern and Northern Pacific virtually dominated the nearby port of Seattle, and access to the busy docks and a suitable location for a large yard in Seattle, with attendant shop facilities, would be most difficult to come by. The Northern Pacific had chosen Tacoma first as its terminus, built a headquarters in Tacoma and then, as Seattle grew in importance, shifted the center of its operations to Seattle. Finally, Tacoma, anxious for a major transcontinental to headquarter in the city, offered both a favorable economic and political climate.

The tide flats of Tacoma, a waste of mud and rank grass, inundated by every tide change and periodically flooded by the Puyallup River, was chosen as the terminal site. Thousands of log pilings were driven into the sooft oozy mud to serve as the foundations for bulkheads, and hundreds of thousands of yards of rock riprap stiffened and raised the banks of the Puyallup River. The seaward edges of the great fill were composed of millions of cubic feet of sand pumped up from Commencement Bay and the outlet of the Puyallup River into the bay. A huge terminal yard and shop facilities were constructed on the high fill. The two wide peninsulas formed, extended out into the bay about two thirds of a mile, and Milwaukee Dock number 1, built in 1909, could accommodate any deep sea vessels. The dock was extended to a length of nine hundred sixty feet and a width of one hundred seventy-five feet, and Milwaukee Dock number 2 was built early in World War I.

AN OLD MALLET COMPOUND alternately barks and whooshes, (from its high and low pressure cylinders), upgrade on the Cedar Falls branch toward the main line junction at Cedar Falls. The slender steel of the Cedar Falls branch, well suited to the slow and light footed Mallets, is today the domain of the equally light footed SD7's.

Stuart B. Hertz

THE OLYMPIAN ON short line bridge between St. Paul and Minneapolis, 1914.

Edward W. Nolan

THE OLYMPIAN ENROUTE Chicago to Seattle and Tacoma, 1914.

Edward W. Nolan

Quickly following the completion of the terminal in Tacoma, the Milwaukee gained access to Grays Harbor at Aberdeen and Hoquiam, still a large lumber producing and export area, by joint track with the Oregon Washington Railroad & Navigation Company. The Tacoma Eastern Railroad Company was leased for access to more lumber producing areas in the Cascades and Mt. Rainier National Park.

Freight service between Mobridge and Butte was started in August, 1908, and passenger service on this section in October. The last spike was driven at Garrison, west of Deer Lodge, on May 14, 1909. Through freight service to the coast began on July 4, 1909, local passenger service on July 10, 1910 (one train a day each way), and the Olympian and Columbian began operation on May 28, 1911.

Just fifty miles from Vancouver, B.C., in the far northwest corner of the state, the city of Bellingham on Puget Sound, had plumped hard for the Milwaukee as a terminus. The city pledged $1,000,000 in land and bonus if the Milwaukee would come to Bellingham, and envisioned not only a vast rail terminal, but Milwaukee docks and a Milwaukee owned steamship line, too. The Great Northern had just such an arrangement. It owned its own docks in Seattle, and two 28,000 ton modern combination passenger/cargo steamships, the Dakota and the

Minnesota, that served the Orient. The Bellingham proposal went for naught, but the Milwaukee did acquire control in 1911, of the Bellingham Bay & British Columbia Rail Road Company in Bellingham. The short line, originally, had been built to haul coal from the local mines to tidewater, and then was extended to the small towns of Lynden, Sumas and Glacier. Service from Bellingham to Seattle was via the Milwaukee Seagoing Railway, a barge line, the land connection with Bellingham being controlled by lines of the Great Northern and Northern Pacific.

The Milwaukee began its Seagoing Railroad, a contracted tug and barge operation, in 1909. It ran across Elliott Bay between terminal trackage in the south end of Seattle and the shingle and lumber mills of Ballard in the north end of the city. The operation was necessitated by the lack of a direct rail link to Ballard, because the existing trackage was all controlled by the Great Northern and Northern Pacific. In 1913, when the 118' steel hulled, 900 horsepower tug Milwaukee was built, the operation was extended up Puget Sound to Bellingham, and across the Sound to Port Townsend, on the Olympic Peninsula, with calls as business dictated, to Eagle Harbor and the Navy Shipyard at Bremerton. Launching of the Milwaukee, the largest tug on the Pacific Coast, was a gala occasion with officials of the road present for the ceremonies.

Operation up and across the Sound was on a tri-weekly basis, with an eleven hour schedule to Bellingham and a six hour schedule to Port Townsend. The seven barges, used to transport the railcars, ranged in size from 100' carrying two cars, to 330' with a 43' beam carrying twenty-one cars. The tides in Puget Sound, rather than a railroad timetable, determined the loading and unloading of the barges. With a tide variation of twenty feet between highs and lows, special floating landing aprons were constructed that would rise and fall with the tide, at Bellingham, Port Townsend and Seattle, so that there would be little interruption of service. Switch engines then were able, regardless of the tides, to reach directly onto the barges to move cars on or off. As one crew member put it, however, "Moving a sixty to ninety ton loaded car from barge to dock trackage, across a floating ramp, is like petting a porcupine — it is done very carefully."

Two seven man crews plus a cook alternate in the service with seven days on and seven days off, standing watches while enroute, and continuous duty when loading or unloading. Barges are towed either singly or in tandem at the end of an 800' to 1,200' steel cable, depending on the weather, with an additional 120' line between the two barges. The tug, Milwaukee, was retired in 1955, after logging 1,600,000 miles between Bellingham, Port Townsend and Seattle. After its retirement, the towing service was contracted to Foss Tug and Barge Company, which operates the service today, using Milwaukee Terminal Company barges.

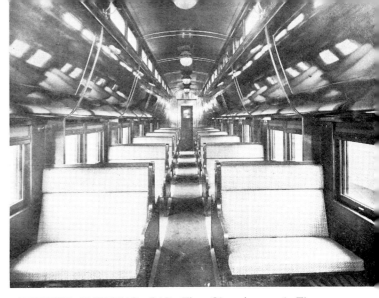

TOURIST SLEEPING CAR The Olympian and The Columbian.

Edward W. Nolan

STANDARD SLEEPING CAR The Olympian and The Columbian.

Edward W. Nolan

DINING CAR THE Olympian, The Columbian, 1914.
Edward W. Nolan

LEAVING TACOMA FOR NORTON, Washington on the old Tacoma & Eastern in 1941, a venerable 2-6-6-2 Mallet compound, engine No. 90, plods its way up the stiff eastbound grade not far from the original Tacoma passenger station. Engine 90 was not rebuilt and simpled as was done on the same class of engines that operated in Eastern Washington. Too slow for main line service, they were usually confined to the branches, where their power and flexibility could be used to advantage.

W. R. McGee

IN THE FLAT PRAIRIE COUNTRY of western Minnesota, and across the line into the Dakota's, wind driven snow often piled deep in cuts. Dry powdery snow could usually be handled by pilot mounted snowplows without too much difficulty, but wet heavy snow that compacted and froze hard was quite another matter, and called for sterner measures, such as this heavily ballasted gondola mounted snowplow. Bucking snow with this rig, and two or three engines, was dangerous work. As the engines charged at the drifts, expert throttle handling was called for to protect the lead engine's crew in case the plow derailed.

Collection of Roger Lins

To St. Paul
and
Minneapolis

The Train of Perfect Equipment on the Road of Perfect Service

The Pioneer Limited

From Chicago in Two Sections — Daily at 6:30 p. m.

Enjoy the travel luxuries and comforts of this famous train — the supreme dining car service — the "longer — higher — wider" berths — the smooth, well-ballasted, double track roadbed. Both sections have compartment, drawing room, standard sleeping cars, buffet smoking cars, dining cars and coaches. *Minneapolis* section arrives St. Paul 6:30 a. m., Minneapolis 7:10 a. m. — *St. Paul* section arrives St. Paul 7:05 a. m., Minneapolis 7:45 a. m., via the

CHICAGO
Milwaukee & St. Paul
RAILWAY

Four other daily trains between Chicago and the Twin Cities

F. A. MILLER
Gen'l Passenger Agent
CHICAGO

51

A SHOTGUN STACKED MOGUL pulling the "Bozeman local" chuffs softly under the catenary just outside of Three Forks, Montana on a hot July day in 1941. Three Forks is aptly named for it lies near the junction of the Madison, Gallatin, and Jefferson Rivers that join to become the Missouri River or "Big Muddy," that along with the Mississippi River forms the largest river system in North America, 3,710 miles in length, draining nearly half the continental United States.

W. R. McGee

WHITE SULPHUR SPRINGS AND YELLOWSTONE Park 4-4-0 No. 36 photographed in February, 1942. The WSS&YP is a twenty-five mile branch line from Ringling, Montana to Dorsey, built in 1910, owned but not operated by the railroad.

W. R. McGee

OUT ON THE HIGH DESOLATE plains of central Montana, between Great Falls and Lewistown, a pair of old Mikes, 626 and 651, struggle with tonnage destined for the main line connection at Harlowton.

W. R. McGee

THROWING A CLOUD OF dark coal smoke back over the high cars, a vestibule cabbed Northern pounds up the approach to the bridge crossing over the Northern Pacific at Terry, Montana, Another bridge then swings the Milwaukee tracks over to the west bank of the Yellowstone River, while the paralleling Northern Pacific heads west along the east bank of the Yellowstone.

W. R. McGee

MILWAUKEE 0-6-0, WITH RUDIMENTARY "main line" pilot — unusual for a switcher — was used for switching in Bozeman and Bozeman-Menard line.

Philip C. Johnson

AN EASTBOUND NORTHERN PACIFIC Mullan branch freight is about to enter the Milwaukee main line, from Haugan to St. Regis, under trackage rights. Much of highway US 10, from Haugan to St. Regis, is on the old Northern Pacific right-of-way wiped out by flood in 1933, and never rebuilt by the Northern Pacific.

Philip C. Johnson

OIL BURNING CLASS S3 Northern 267 leads a westbound freight across PeeDee viaduct, above Chatcolet Lake, in 1957. PeeDee, Idaho is located between St. Maries and Plummer Junction, not far from Lake Couer d'Alene, in some of the most rugged and beautiful country in the Northwest.

Philip C. Johnson

WITH BELL RINGING, PACIFIC Number 889 thumps across the Great Northern track and Sherman Avenue (main street) in Coeur d'Alene, Idaho, in 1951. Steam power was rare on the Coeur d'Alene branch in the 1950's, most traffic being handled by light diesels out of Spokane.

Philip C. Johnson

MALLET NUMBER 50, ONE OF the modernized 2-6-6-2's, turns on the wye after bringing train Number 102 over the hill from Bovill on the Idaho Division Fourth Subdivision, which is essentially a logging branch.
Dr. Philip R. Hastings

MILWAUKEE STEAM POWERED LOG train, 2-8-0 No. 1214, was photographed in 1947 near Bovill, on the run over the St. Maries branch from Elk River to Bovill and St. Maries.
Philip C. Johnson

2-8-0 NUMBER 1229, WITH SOUTHBOUND freight 103, meets 2-6-6-2 Number 50, with northbound freight 102, on the Fourth Subdivision to Elk River. Number 1229 will turn to take 102 on to St. Maries, and Number 50 will turn to lead 103 to Bovill.

Dr. Philip R. Hastings

L2 MIKE NO. 687, in helper service, waits at Plummer Junction, where the main line freight and passenger line into Spokane diverge.

Dr. Philip R. Hastings

A MILWAUKEE EXTRA WEST, behind 4-6-2 No. 889, makes its way into Spokane across the long, high Union Pacific trestle that crosses the Spokane River Valley. *(opposite)*

Dr. Philip R. Hastings

L2 2-8-2 NO. 711, ASSIGNED TO A work extra laying steel on the First Subdivision of the Idaho Division, crosses a stout framed bent trestle at Rosalia, Washington, in 1950.

Dr. Philip R. Hastings

N-3 2-6-6-2 NO. 58 ROLLS FREIGHT 291 north, up the beautiful Pend Oreille River Valley on the Metalline Falls Branch. The Branch reaches almost to the Canadian border, but does not interchange with the Canadian Pacific Railroad.

Dr. Philip R. Hastings

THE MILWAUKEE Road established trade connections with the Orient in August, 1909, when the Japanese ship Tacoma Maru arrived at the Tacoma docks with 500 tons of cargo to be transshipped to the east via the Milwaukee Road. Over the years this traffic steadily increased, and this 1949 picture of the main yard of the road and the docks, illustrates the importance of transportation to the city of Tacoma.

Tacoma News Tribune

A MILWAUKEE "SEATRAIN," enroute to Port Townsend and Bellingham, crosses Elliott Bay behind a Foss tug. The only railroad barge service in the Northwest, it has been in daily service since 1913.

Port of Seattle

THE STEAM POWERED TUG MILWAUKEE moves into the east waterway passing Harbor Island enroute to the barge terminal.

The Milwaukee Road

THE CAPTAIN OF A Foss tug prepares to move a Milwaukee rail barge out into Elliott Bay from the waterfront terminal. During short moves, or with only one barge, the tug is often lashed to the barge, as maneuvering is simpler than towing.

Port of Seattle

Chapter III

ELECTRIFICATION

In 1907, while much of the western extension was still under construction, officers of the Milwaukee publicly stated that an electrification project in the formidable Bitter Roots "was under advisement." Rumors to this effect had persisted for some time, probably occasioned by land purchasing agents of the Milwaukee, who not only had bought land for the right-of-way and timber lands in the name of the Milwaukee Land Company — 450,000 acres worth $20,000,000 in Washington and Idaho — but also had bought land for electrical development — substations and generating plants. Further, flow rights had been negotiated for on the St. Joe River in Idaho, and eleven dams were planned with a total capacity of 180,000 horsepower. The Milwaukee then, was considering not only electrifying a portion of the railroad, but building its own generating plants, dams and distribution network as well — a tremendous undertaking.

There were some fine examples of electrification, on the Pennsylvania among others, over short distances, but electrification of a considerable distance of main line had never been done. Electrification had been used mainly to overcome tunnel and smoke nuisance problems within metropolitan areas, and this provided insufficient data with which to make a judgement on the feasibility of electrifying a whole division or more. An important consideration, was the availability of power. Although the states of Idaho and Montana were growing rapidly, Montana in 1907, had a total capacity in its existing hydroelectric plants of only about 25,000 kw, an amount far short of that needed by the railroad, to say nothing of other users of the power. It would be a very expensive proposition, however, for the railroad to build its own generating and distribution network, since it would be needed at full capacity only about ten percent of the time to serve the peak load demands of the railroad. Of further consideration was the dependability of hydroelectric power as a source of power. There was excess power to be had during the late spring and early summer, as the snow pack melted and the streams ran brim full, but what would happen during dry seasons when the rivers and streams flow rate was very low? How much storage capacity, in how many watersheds would be needed to insure adequate water power to turn the generators and produce the electricity needed?

Into this situation stepped John D. Ryan, elected to the board of directors of the Milwaukee Road in 1909, after the death of Henry H. Rogers. Rogers had been in the Rockefeller "camp," and his successor was selected at the suggestion of William Rockefeller. The board recognized the importance of selecting a man from the West, familiar with the vast western reaches the Milwaukee now covered, and could not have made a better choice than John D. Ryan, president of the powerful Anaconda Copper Mining Company. Rockefeller held a large block of stock in the company, but far more important from the railroad's point of view, was Ryan's experience with the problems that Anaconda had had in the mines with steam powered pumps and blowers, problems that were finally resolved through the use of electric power. Ryan also was a director of Great Falls Power Company and Thompson Falls Power Company (the predecessors of Montana Power). He had

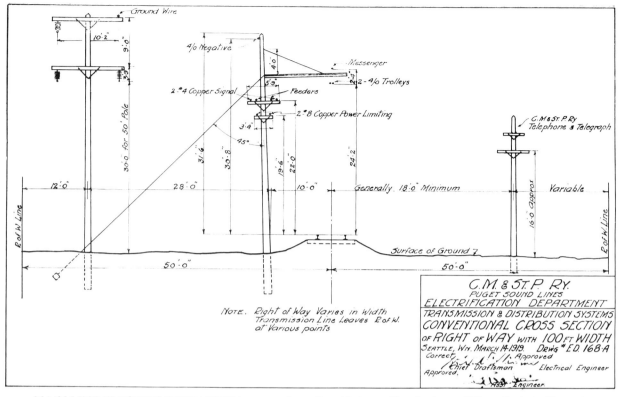

MAIN LINE ELECTRIC OPERATION began on the railroad between Deer Lodge and Three Forks in November, 1915, but the earliest electric operation on the road actually began March 31, 1915 when switcher 10000 went into service in Falls Yard. Operation was limited to a small area in Great Falls, with no evidence of plans to extend electrification from the main line further south to Great Falls.

The Milwaukee Road

been in on the development of hydroelectric generating plants on Montana rivers, and in the development of long distance high voltage transmission lines, that brought cheap and reliable power to the mines and other consumers. Anaconda had worked hand in hand with the power companies in the initial development of this project to the satisfaction of Anaconda and of individual users of the power. With his interlocking interest in copper, electric power and railroads, Ryan was well able to serve and guide the Milwaukee in its plans for electrification.

In 1909, another western railroad used electrification to solve its problems in the steep Cascades. The Great Northern had completed 2.63 mile long Cascade Tunnel, in 1900, after operating for seven years over a series of 4% grade switchbacks that were not only dangerous, but served as a bottleneck to traffic flowing east and west. It was thought that the new tunnel, which eliminated these switchbacks and reduced the ruling gradient to 2.2%, would solve the problem, but a new problem was created. A tonnage train working slowly upgrade, between Wellington and Cascade Tunnel Station, created so much smoke and gas in the tunnel, that the crews were subject to intense heat and near suffocation. Passengers, too, complained of the accumulated smoke and gas seeping into the cars, and several tragedies were narrowly averted, when a train stalled in the tunnel, managed to back out just in time.

The problem was solved with a three-phase electrification system between Wellington and Cascade Tunnel Station, that allowed electric locomotives to pull entire trains, with their steam engines (but not working steam), through the tunnel. It was a fairly simple operation, and it worked so well that the Great Northern was already considering electrifying an entire division to take advantage of the economies of electric operation. The Great Northern owned its own generating plant at Tumwater, on the Wenatchee River.

This operation did not pass unnoticed by the Milwaukee, also experiencing much difficulty with steam power in the mountains. Complaints were heard from passengers and crews, particularly in the Bitter Roots on the steep grade from Haugan to Avery, where the road was one tunnel after another, and the cars and engines filled with cindery smoke and gas. Nevertheless, no major railroad had entered into an electrification program to make that electrification stand solely on its own merits, rather than as an adjunct to steam power. That is, the economies effected by electric operation — elimination of coaling docks, water plugs and ash pits, the around the clock availability of power, less wear and tear on equipment, and longer trains with fewer crews — should make the high initial investment pay for itself by returning more money to the road through the more efficient operation of the trains.

There were other reasons that the road considered turning to electric power to run the trains. While the Milwaukee owned a coal (lignite) mine at Roundup, Montana, it did not, as the Northern Pacific did, own coal mines in Idaho and Washington, and transporting coal hundreds of miles was expensive.

The Milwaukee operated through Benewah and Shoshone counties in Idaho, and Mineral County in Montana, a part of the vast area that had burned in a terrible forest fire near Avery, Idaho, in 1910. The fire had reached into northern Idaho and northwestern Montana, raging nearly five hundred miles north to Canada, and as a result, laws were passed to prohibit the use of both coal and wood burning locomotives in the Idaho Forest Preserve. Although the Milwaukee was not responsible for starting the fire, its operations were affected. Steam locomotives, operating in Idaho, Washington and western Montana, had to be converted to burn oil, which was even more costly than coal and had to be transported great distances. Oil was coming into more general usage throughout the country, and the already high price of oil, was rising steadily. With inexpensive horsepower available in the raging rivers of the northwest, right beside the main line in many places, why not put it to use?

Ryan readily convinced President Earling and other members of the board, that the Milwaukee would be far better off utilizing the expanded commercial facilities already in existence, than to em-

ON EXHIBITION IN BUTTE, Montana at the Butte Anaconda & Pacific station, box cab 10200 is spotted between BA & P 66 on the left and 6501 of the Milwaukee Road on the right. The 2400 volt DC catenary of the BA & P was used for a successful demonstration even though the 10200 had been designed to use 3,000 volt DC.

The Milwaukee Road

bark on a costly construction program of its own. The power generating capacity of Montana and Washington Power Companies was doubling and tripling, every few years, as demand for electric power increased. The year around availability of hydroelectric power, regardless of the weather, was provided by the use of many watersheds and inter-connected transmission systems. There was, therefore, little reason to believe that the Milwaukee would ever be caught short of "white coal" when it was needed.

A further argument in favor of electrification was the disappointing performance of steam power on the mountain grades, particularly in the winter time. The steam power that had been adequate to operate the railroad across the five mountain ranges

when the road was opened for through freight service on the 4th of July, 1909, was strained when the tonnage reached 1,500,000 tons, barely a year later. By the middle of 1911, the annual tonnage hauled reached 2,500,000 tons. The Milwaukee invested over $8,000,000, between 1909 and 1914, in new steam locomotives (including two hundred new Mikado freight types) built primarily for service from Minneapolis to the Pacific Coast, in an effort to keep up with the rising tonnage hauled.

In the mountain districts, the situation became critical. Ascending the 1.66% grade east of Butte to the summit of the Continental Divide at Donald, seventeen miles away, moving a two thousand ton train, required three Mikado type locomotives, three engineers, three firemen, brakemen and a conduc-

THE FIRST ELECTRIC FREIGHT motor built for the Milwaukee, GE No. 10200 A & B is on display in Butte before entering service.

The Milwaukee Road

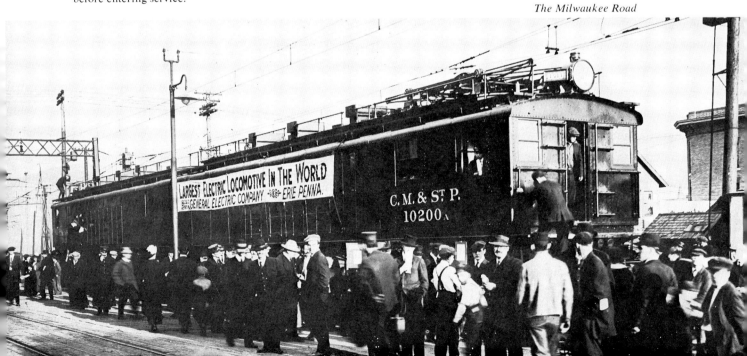

MUCH HEAVY CONSTRUCTION ON the railroad was completed during 1914 and 1915. Temporary trackage was rebuilt, heavy steel bridges were constructed, and fills over trestlework shook down and stabilized. Here a steam shovel and air hammers are utilized to widen a narrow cut and to remove the loose and overhanging rock.

The Milwaukee Road

AUTOMATIC BLOCK SIGNALS guard the newly electrified main line of the railroad in Montana in 1915. A pioneer in the development and use of ABS, the Milwaukee Road was among the first railroads in the Northwest to use them.

The Milwaukee Road

tor. It also required tons of coal, thousands of gallons of water, and nearly two hours time — if all went well. Once through Pipestone Pass tunnel at the top, the train stopped while the retainers on the cars were set up to assist in the braking while descending the twenty-one miles of 2% grade to Piedmont. At this point, the two helper locomotives, with no more useful work to do, could either be cut off to return to Butte or continue on down with the train. The train, with the air brakes partially set to prevent losing control on the grade, proceeded slowly on down the mountain, with another lengthy stop or two to let the brakes and wheels cool. With this operation repeated on other mountain grades at Haugan, Harlowton, Cle Elum, Cedar Falls and Avery, the number of locomotives and crews needed to keep just the freight moving was fast getting out of hand. Add to this situation, delays, bad weather, minor accidents, break downs, locomotives low on fuel and water, passenger train schedules that had to be kept, and the entire road could be in a snarl from one end to the other.

In late 1910 and early 1911, the Milwaukee put twenty-five Mallet compound locomotives into service to assist as pushers on the heaviest grades. Eleven more super heated versions followed in 1912. Theoretically capable of moving nearly a thousand tons up the steepest grades at six to eight miles per hour, they were supposed to be over half

again as powerful as the early Mikados. In actuality, they were the biggest single motive power headache the operating department had yet to face. In service, the big Mallets quickly proved to be notorious steam hogs, even using steam while drifting down a 1% grade. Firemen couldn't keep them hot when they were working hard, and they rarely developed full rated power. They leaked steam around every flexible joint in both the high and low pressure steam systems around the rear and front cylinders. In the winter time, the leaking steam condensed, dripped down onto the railhead, and promptly froze the locomotive to the rails, immobilizing the entire train until help could be called to break them loose.

The Mallets were not the only locomotives adversely affected by the bitter winter weather in Montana and the Dakotas. Every steam locomotive lost some of the boiler heat by radiation in the sub-zero temperatures (-30 and -40 degrees was not uncommon). Grease and oil stiffened in the car journals to a taffy like consistency, and extra power was needed to urge the tonnage into motion. Steam heated passenger equipment required more heat from the locomotive boiler, and double-heading of passenger trains was necessary, on even the lighter grades, to keep a tight schedule. These factors combined to reduce tonnage ratings by 25 to 30%.

A SUBSTATION UNDER CONSTRUCTION in one of the beautiful valleys of Montana.

The Milwaukee Road

A LINE CAR SITS ON THE main line just beyond the turnout at Colorado Junction where the Butte Anaconda & Pacific tracks join those of the Milwaukee Road. In the background, the ramparts of the Rocky Mountains rise above the valley. Butte, by night, is transformed into a glittering myriad of lights from the city and the surrounding mines that can be seen for miles in the clear cold air.

The Milwaukee Road

The continual slack action, as trains were jerked into motion on the many grades, caused rapid wear and frequent failure of the draft gear on the freight equipment. Power had to be changed every one hundred miles or so — a common steam practice — with locomotives out of service for long periods for servicing and maintenance. Even under the best conditions, operation was generally slow, unwieldy and expensive.

There was an electrification program begun in Montana, in 1911, to replace an entire existing steam operation, that was to deeply influence the Milwaukee in its decision to undertake the electrification of the road in the three far western states. On the doorstep of the Milwaukee, the Butte Anaconda & Pacific Railway, a subsidiary of the Anaconda Company, completed its electrification in 1913. In 1909, the steam powered Butte Anaconda & Pacific was experiencing a tremendous growth in tonnage hauled, as the demand for copper increased steadily. Operating only some seventy miles of railroad, the BA&P at first glance, would seem to have very little in common with the Milwaukee. However, its main line, though only twenty-six miles long between the mines at Butte and the smelter at Anaconda, was moving thousands of tons of ore on a regularly scheduled basis, sixteen hours a day throughout the year. Grades on the main ranged from 1 to 2.5%. On the "hill" at Butte, serving the mines, twenty-five miles of track twisted in every possible direction through curves as sharp as 22 degrees and grades as steep as 4%. The well maintained Consolidations and Twelve Wheelers, that made up the largest portion of the locomotive roster, were increasingly hard pressed to keep up with the rising tonnage. The railroad could either rebuild the road and buy new heavier steam power to meet the increased demand, or consider some alternate source of power. One such alternative was a conveyer belt, another was electric power.

Electric "Mules" were powering the little trains down in the mines, and the electric motors, pumps and generators in wide use in the mines and at the smelter, had proven themselves to be economical, reliable and virtually maintenance free. Anaconda Company already had two substations, one at the mine and one at the smelter, suitable for installation of the motor-generators to convert the power from the transmission lines. A completely electrified railroad would use literally hundreds of tons of Anaconda copper in the overhead trolley, power lines and locomotives. If successful, the promotion, publicity and sales value of the electrification would be of enormous benefit to the Anaconda, the future development and growth of power companies, and to the supplier of the electric locomotives.

General Electric Company experts were called in to study the situation and to advise the Butte Anaconda & Pacific. The General Electric people concluded that a heavy duty installation, such as the

67

A FLASH PHOTOGRAPH OF THE interior of the construction engineer's car, in 1915, during the building of the electrification in Montana, shows drafting tools, map cases, a transit, and other assorted instruments, papers and books scattered about the car, and a turn of the century "pin-up" decorating the far wall.

The Milwaukee Road

Butte Anaconda & Pacific needed, should be a 2400 volt DC system that offered advantages in transmission of the power, fewer substations, lower initial cost of the feeders, and lower operating cost due to improved pick-up from the trolley by the locomotives. General Electric had pioneered a very successful commutating pole DC motor that was rugged in construction and simple to control. Similar in design to the Great Northern units in the Cascades, the locomotives were short, rather stumpy, eighty-one ton units of B-B wheel arrangement, designed to run in multiple or as single units. A pair of them were slightly lighter than a steam road engine and tender, but were half again as powerful. They were flexible enough to follow any trackage or curves on Butte "hill" serving the mine spurs, where it had been necessary to use 0-6-0 switchers with the steam road engines restricted largely to the main lines. Seventeen units were delivered in 1913, with more to follow, and the twenty-seven steam engines were sold or scrapped at a later date.

General Electric engineers had calculated that the initial cost of the electrification would be about one and one quarter million dollars, and that due to cheaper operating costs and increased efficiency, the return on the investment would be about seventeen percent. After the first year of operation, the actual return amounted to almost twenty-one percent. Primary reasons for the large return were:

three electric locomotives did the work of four steamers; one crew could do the work of two; the locomotives ran for two shifts — sixteen hours — per day with only light servicing. Savings in fuel alone accounted for $150,000, and annual net savings in crews and reduced maintenance costs amounted to another $100,000, for a total net savings of over a quarter million dollars. As a result, the road paid for itself in five — not six years.

The outstanding success of the Butte Anaconda & Pacific, measured by any technological or economic yardstick a critic might wish to apply, caused an immediate reaction in railroad circles. As work on the Butte Anaconda & Pacific progressed, information on that work went directly to President Earling from the president of Anaconda Company. The Milwaukee already had begun a detailed electrification study in 1912, under the direction of C. A. Goodnow, who reported directly to President Earling and electrical engineer Reiner Beeuwkes. In the same year, the Milwaukee announced its decision to electrify the one hundred thirteen mile stretch of road between Deer Lodge and Three Forks, (through Butte and over the Continental Divide), and through Mr. Ryan, negotiated a ninety-nine year contract with Great Falls Power Company for electric power to serve the Rocky Mountain Division. In 1913, the Milwaukee entered into a similar contract with Thompson Falls Power Company for the Missoula Division. The two companies merged soon after, to become Montana Power Company, with a total capacity of over 70,000 kw. of hydroelectric power, plus a small stand-by capacity in steam plants. Montana Power had been gathering information too, from several sources, and had started to build additional generating plants, in anticipation of the imminent electrification of the Milwaukee. With permission granted, by the Secretary of the Interior of the United States, to Montana Power to build power distribution facilities between Harlowton and Avery, only the formal announcement by the Milwaukee of its intentions to electrify the entire four hundred forty mile stretch of line across the Belt, Rocky and Bitter Root Mountains, was needed to get the electrification program underway.

The Electrification Department of the Milwaukee was formally created March, 1914, with Mr. Goodnow vice-president and Mr. Beeuwkes chief electrical engineer. General Electric was to be the prime supplier of all electrical equipment, and its engineers would serve as technical advisors, working in conjunction with the Electrification Department in the installation and operation of all equipment. American Locomotive Company would build the General Electric designed locomotives, with General Electric supplying the motors and other electrical components. Montana Power, by enlarging existing hydroelectric generating facilities, and by developing new plants, mainly on the Missouri River, would furnish 100,000 volt, three-phase alternating current to the fourteen Milwaukee Road substations between Harlowton and Avery. The new 35,000 kw. plant at Thompson Falls, on the Clark Fork of the Columbia was the primary supplier to the west end of the electrification. Enlarged existing facilities on the Missouri and the new 60,000 kw. plant, due to be completed in 1916, at the Great Falls of the Missouri, supplied the eastern end of the Electrification at Harlowton.

The railroad built several hundred miles of 100,000 volt power lines to connect the more remote substations. At the substations, the 100,000 volt alternating current was reduced by transformers to 2,300 volts, and converted by motor generators to 3,000 volt direct current, for distribution over a catenary trolley system, suspended normally twenty-four feet above the running rails. The 3,000 volt direct current running power, was the highest pressure yet used by a railroad. The design of the Milwaukee system closely followed the basic design of the Butte Anaconda & Pacific, which ran successfully on 2,400 volts direct current. Unlike those of the Butte Anaconda & Pacific, however, the new Milwaukee locomotives were designed with a regenerative braking system that allowed the locomotives to hold back a train, while descending grades, with the resistance built up as the motors — turned into generators — fed current back into the catenary. It proved so successful that every electric locomotive built from this date on, for use on mountain grades, incorporated regenerative braking. The system was also the ancestor of the equally effective dynamic braking, used on diesel locomotives years later.

On November 24, 1914, the first contract for forty-two locomotives (twelve passenger and thirty freight) and equipment was signed, and one year later on November 30, 1915 at 9:05 A.M., the trolley wire was energized for the first time between Butte and Eustis Substation, at the foot of the grade on the east side of the Rockies. Power was supplied from the substations at Janney (near Butte) and

THESE WELL BUILT BUNGALOWS were typical employee quarters at the substations. The "Chic Sales" behind the bungalows were responsible for establishing some fast track records during the frigid winters in Idaho and Montana.

The Milwaukee Road

A 3,000 VOLT DIRECT current switchboard at Piedmont substation.

The Milwaukee Road

THE TRANSFORMER ROOM of the substation at Morel, Montana shows the three phase 100,000-2,300 volt transformers and oil circuit breakers.

The Milwaukee Road

Piedmont on the east slope. At 10:20 A.M., locomotive 10200, with business car Walworth and caboose 0801 in tow, moved eastward from Three Forks eight miles to Eustis, and then reversed to run west, up and across the Continental Divide to Butte. Proclaimed "the largest electric locomotive in the world," 10200 had been received by the road on September 15th, and left Chicago on October 6th for an exhibition tour along the line to Tacoma. On its return it was tested briefly on the rails of the Butte Anaconda & Pacific. On December 1, 1915, the trolley was energized between Butte and Deer Lodge, and 10200, with the same train in tow as on the preceeding day, made the round trip.

After the first trial runs with locomotive 10200, the tonnage pulled was gradually increased, until on

December 6, 1915, a train of 2,800 tons was taken from Butte yard with locomotive 10201 on the point and 10200 pushing. This heavy train ran up the 1.66% grade from Butte to Donald at a steady fifteen miles per hour. At Donald, locomotive 10200 ran around the train, and coupled on ahead with locomotive 10201, to assist with the regenerative braking. Moving down the east slope, the two locomotives, by regenerative braking, dropped the train down the mountain at a steady seventeen miles per hour. Upon completion of the trip, the two locomotives required nothing but train orders to return to service immediately — quite a change from the steam power that would have required turning, coaling, watering, ash pans cleaned, and probably adjustments before returning to service.

A 2,000 KW., 3,000 VOLT direct current synchronous motor-generator set is being installed in one of the substations in Montana.

The Milwaukee Road

IN DECEMBER, 1915 A WESTBOUND 1,450 ton freight train, behind motor 10211, posed at Donald, Montana — summit of the Continental Divide in the Rocky Mountains.

General Electric Company

On December 7, 1915, the Olympian was hauled by locomotive 10200 (a freight locomotive) from Butte to Three Forks, making the schedule without difficulty. Passengers aboard, commented favorably on the remarkable smoothness of the operation, and on the freedom from smoke and cinders. Wednesday, December 8th, President Earling and the board of directors arrived from the east to inspect the property and to watch the operation of substation machinery. Along with a delegation from the Butte Chamber of Commerce, they witnessed a demonstration of two freight trains in action — one steam and one electric powered. The movement of these trains can best be described by the words of Butte newspapers of December 9, 1915.

"The test consisted of starting from Butte a train of 3,000 tons, consisting of 48 loaded cars pulled by two electric locomotives, and the train was hauled over the grade quietly and apparently with the utmost ease at a speed of 16 mph, and proceeded on its eastern way without stopping. Following behind this train came another of 2,000 tons made up of 37 cars hauled by two "L" engines and pushed by a mallet locomotive. The steam horses toiled up the grade and the engines actually groaned under the strain placed upon them. The men at the throttles and the firemen shoveling coal were not trying to throw the race, but it was quite apparent that they had a pride in making the best possible show for their iron steeds, and steam was kept at the highest possible pressure, yet with the smaller tonnage the three locomotives made hard work on the grade and only managed to get through Janney at a speed of nine miles an hour."

"There was something almost pathetic in the game fight which steam put up against its new rival

ELECTRIC MOTORS RIDE THE turntable in Deer Lodge where just short months before, the Iron Ponies held the reins. While the steamers failed in the ability to make steam or keep it up due to bitter cold weather conditions, the big electrics benefitted from the cold temperatures that cooled the traction motors and markedly increased their efficiency.

The Milwaukee Road

CARRYING GREEN FLAGS ON her pilot beam, freight motor 10204a joins forces with her sister 10204b on 2,680 tons westbound in Silver Bow Canyon. Some of the freight motors, brand spanking new in this 1915 photograph, are still in extra service in the Cascades, and as helpers in the Rocky Mountains in 1971.

General Electric Company

in the transportation field, but it was so visibly and completely outclassed that even a child could have picked the easy winner at a glance. Not one of the half hundred spectators could help feeling that he had witnessed the overwhelming triumph of a new power over an old and tried friend that had faithfully served mankind for many decades past."

Early in 1917, full service was inaugurated between Avery and Harlowton, nearly a year ahead of schedule. This operation proved to be so successful, that work on the two hundred eight mile Coast Division between Othello and Tacoma was started

almost immediately, and was completed in November, 1919. Twelve re-geared General Electric passenger locomotives were transferred to the Coast Division for freight service, and five Bi-polars were ordered for passenger service. The General Electric locomotives were replaced on the Rocky Mountain Division with ten Baldwin-Westinghouse locomotives for passenger service. Originally it had been planned to electrify the entire road from Harlowton to Tacoma, and the railroad held an option on power for the Idaho Division from Avery to Othello until 1921. However, because of the absence of heavy

Tonnage hauled by the Milwaukee electrics climbed steadily to a peak in 1920, of 3,402,419,000 gross ton miles. Unfortunately, due to many factors, from this point tonnage declined, and it became increasingly difficult for the road to make payments on its bonds. The investment of some $23,000,000 in the electrification program — $15,000,000 in the Rockies and $9,000,000 in the Cascades — was not the main cause of the bankruptcy of the road in 1925, however. In fact, the $12,400,000 net savings (as of 1924) made possible by the electrification probably helped to forestall the coming financial difficulties. In the words of Mr. Goodnow, "Our electrification has been tested by the worst winter weather in the memory of modern railroaders. There were times when every steam locomotive in the Rocky Mountain district was frozen, but the electric locomotives went right along. Electrification has in every way exceeded our expectations. This is so, not only as respects tonnage handled and mileage made, but also the regularity of operation."

The units delivered to the road in the second decade of the Twentieth Century are now, after millions of miles of service, just about worn out. In the 1950's, the delivery to the road of the twelve "Little Joes" probably saved the electrification from being scrapped in favor of diesel power. Now the hard working "Little Joes," operating in combination with diesel power, are not far from needed replacement, and the road is faced with an evaluation of its electrification. The solution is not a simple one of replacing motive power. The entire electrical system is in need of extensive rebuilding or replacement. Tremendous strides have been made in the last twenty years in alternating current systems that are more efficient and economical than the direct current system used on the Milwaukee. With the growing awareness of the need to protect our environment, a new interest has been awakened on the part of other roads in regard to electric operation. Perhaps the Milwaukee, the pioneer of heavy duty long distance electric operation can lead the way.

grades on this division, and the splitting of traffic — passenger through Spokane for a distance of one hundred twenty miles via Plummer Junction to Marengo, and freight over the through route via Malden — and because of the poor economic conditions, the plan was abandoned. The final bit of electrification was completed in 1926, when the ten mile stretch from Black River Junction into Seattle was put into service, and it was no longer necessary to couple on steam power for the run into Union Station. Seattle then became "the largest city on the longest electrified line in the world."

A BROAD RADIUS CURVE SWINGS THE main line out of the rocky confines of Montana Canyon onto tangent track, as the railroad heads for Deer Park, and then swings again to the left to avoid a direct confrontation with the steeper grades in the high mountains of the Deer Park area.
Asahel Curtis

IN A BEAUTIFUL EXAMPLE of cut, fill, and bridge the BA&P crosses over the Milwaukee and Northern Pacific main lines in Silver Bow Canyon.

The Milwaukee Road

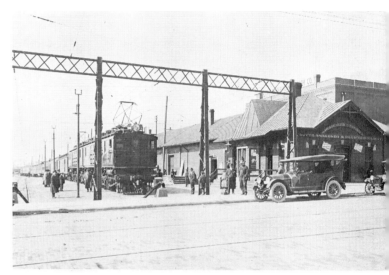

UNTIL THE COMPLETION of the Milwaukee station in Butte, the BA&P station served as a temporary terminal for the Milwaukee. This photograph of the stub end terminal was taken about 1916.

The Milwaukee Road

THE BUTTE, MONTANA passenger station, wholly owned by the Milwaukee Road, was completed in 1917. A stub end terminal, it required either backing into the station or backing out by all passenger trains. The Butte Anaconda & Pacific shared use of the station.

The Milwaukee Road

HIGH ABOVE BUTTE THE main line of the railroad threads its way along the mountain side as if searching for a way down from its high perch. Like the neighboring Northern Pacific, the Milwaukee descends a steep 1.7% grade ten miles long to Butte by a series of spirals and loops, that in many locations, cling to the mountain side and afford a spectacular view of the valley below.

The Milwaukee Road

CONSTRUCTION TRAIN EQUIPMENT LINES the yard at Deer Lodge in 1916 prior to the completion of the electrification program in November. Boxcars bearing the name Chicago Milwaukee and St. Paul dominate the scene, although one car lettered Chicago Milwaukee and Puget Sound is in the foreground. Still to appear is the corporate name, Chicago Milwaukee St. Paul and Pacific.

The Milwaukee Road

OBSERVATION END OF THE Olympian, train 16 — eastbound — at Deer Lodge in 1916.

The Milwaukee Road

EAGLE NEST TUNNEL IN Montana Canyon with Sixteen Mile Creek running below. Wildly beautiful and rugged country, the canyon is virtually uninhabited except for wild game and rattlesnakes by the tens of thousands. Train and section crews working in the area are issued snake-bite kits as a standard precaution.

The Milwaukee Road

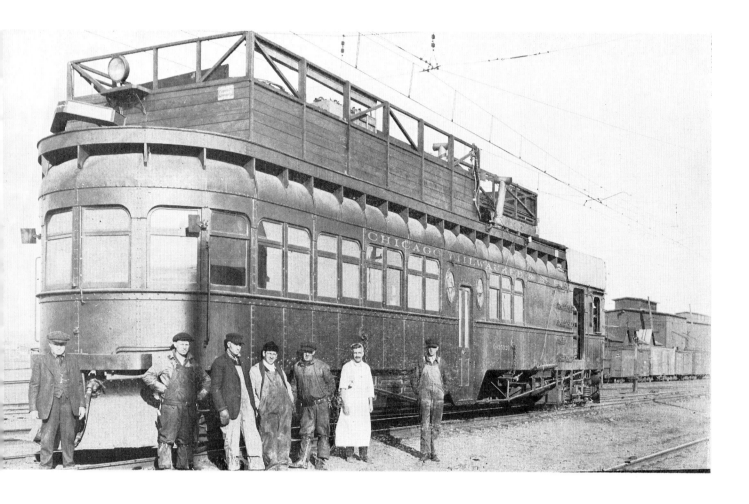

THIS LINE CONSTRUCTION CAR in Montana, modified from a branch line self propelled passenger car, was later used as a trouble-shooter car after completion of the electrification.

The Milwaukee Road

IN THE SUMMER OF 1922, a freight train with four motors on the point, rounded a curve on the mountain side, six hundred feet above Change Creek, near Garcia, Washington, on the way up to Snoqualmie Pass. Before the startled crew could bring the motors to a stop, they hit a rock slide that had carried away the track, but had not broken the catenary. One after the other, the four motors rolled down the mountain side, shedding trucks, frames and other parts. Section gangs and a work crew rebuilt the roadbed and track, and two big hooks moved in to recover the wrecked motors, Today, a Highway 90 East bridge crosses Change Creek at the site of the accident.

Collection of Charles R. Wood

THE OLYMPIAN OF THE MID 1920's, behind a glossy black Baldwin passenger motor, passes through Hell Gate Canyon, close to Missoula, Montana.

Asahel Curtis

COLUMBIA RIVER BRIDGE looking west to the Saddle Mountains.

Collection of Charles R. Wood

AT EAST PORTAL, MONTANA, the summit of the main line in the Bitter Root Mountains and the site of St. Paul Pass tunnel (8,771 feet in length), the snow piles up to astounding depths. It has reached the eves of the company house, and its depth of several feet on the roof makes it necessary to shovel off the excess weight to relieve the strain and danger of collapse.

The Milwaukee Road

IN 1955, THE LAST WINTER of its operation, steam powered rotary X900209 churns through East Portal, Montana while clearing the main and passing siding, just outside the St. Paul Pass tunnel. Its progress is marked by a column of steam and smoke, and by a wall of flying snow along the right of way.

The Milwaukee Road

PULLMAN CAR & Mfg. Co. built "Trouble Shooter" X671, along with car X670, patrolled the overhead catenary from one end of the system to the other. Originally constructed in 1939, the cars were rebuilt in 1945, and were powered with an eight cylinder Winton gas engine. Equipped with a complete kitchen, dining room, four bunks, and a fifteen foot long workshop, the cars and crew were capable of extended trips to maintain or repair the overhead wiring. The cars, which required an engineer, fireman and conductor, have been replaced by rail-highway trucks.

The Milwaukee Road

OLYMPIAN HIAWATHA, TRAIN NO. 16 at Penfield, Montana, climbs the 2% grade to Pipestone Pass behind a Bi-polar, in 1957.

Philip C. Johnson

LEADING AN EXTRA WESTBOUND freight at Cyr, Montana, just west of Alberton, with an additional four unit motor deadheading four cars behind the lead motor, a four unit freight motor rolls out onto Cyr viaduct across the Clark Fork River. Cyr viaduct is one of three bridges of similar size and design that span the Clark Fork in the 43 miles between St. Regis and Alberton.

Philip C. Johnson

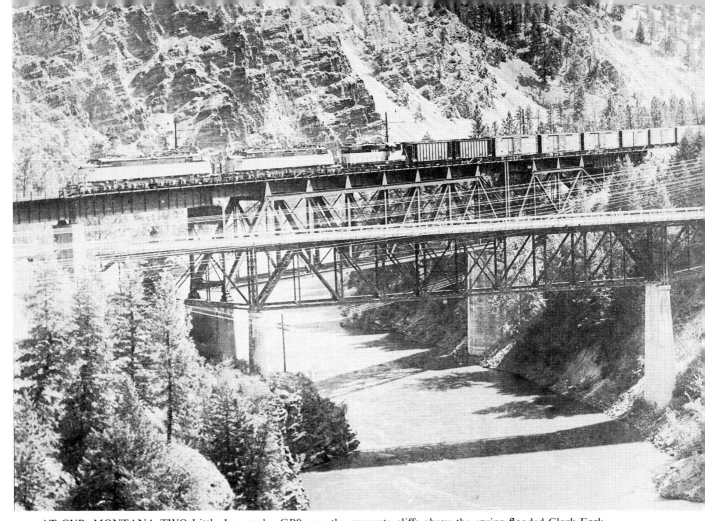

AT CYR, MONTANA TWO Little Joes and a GP9 pass the magenta cliffs above the spring flooded Clark Fork River and the old US 10 highway bridge.

Philip C. Johnson

IN 1950, THE COLUMBIAN, behind all black class EP-3 Baldwin-Westinghouse motor E-17, passes over the tracks of the Northern Pacific freight line (Missoula to Paradise, Montana), and crosses over the Clark Fork River. The train order board, located at the end of the approach fill, is controlled by the Northern Pacific St. Regis station operator, as this stretch of track is used also by the Northern Pacific, under trackage rights, as far as Haugan, Montana, because the Northern Pacific tracks in the St. Regis River canyon were wiped out in the flood of December, 1933.

Philip C. Johnson

AT DONALD, MONTANA, ON the east slope of the Continental Divide, Extra E-54 West climbs the 2% grade with the assistance of a three unit mid-train helper.

Philip C. Johnson

MILWAUKEE TRAIN 16, THE Olympian Hiawatha behind a resplendent Bi-polar, pulls into the then new Butte Station in December, 1957. The new station did away with the necessity of wye-ing trains in and out of the old, more pretentious station, but served the railroad only a few years. With the end of passenger service in May, 1961, it was boarded up.

Philip C. Johnson

Chapter IV

Motive Power

When the Pacific extension of the Milwaukee Road was being planned and built, considerable study was also being given to the types of motive power that would be needed to power the freight and passenger trains between Minneapolis and the Pacific Coast. The road carefully selected motive power suited to the operating conditions imposed by the terrain being crossed. Pulling a tonnage train across the flat prairie country of the Dakotas was far different from pushing and pulling the same train up and across 2% grades of the Belts, Rockies, Bitter Roots, Saddles and Cascades. It was deemed desireable to have power that was capable of pulling tonnage through to the Pacific Coast in solid trains, rather than breaking the train up into smaller units between points involving heavy grades and sharp curves, and yet the length of the run from Minneapolis to Seattle/Tacoma (over 1,800 miles) required fast running where possible — the one objective, pulling power, often inconsistent with the other, speed.

A further complication was the bitter winter weather, both on the prairies and in the mountains, that reduced tonnage, at times, by 30% or more. It became obvious that several types of power would have to be designed and built to suit the varied operating conditions. At the same time, in order to economize and to simplify servicing and repair work, it was also desirable, so far as possible, to build locomotives that would use interchangeable parts. In this way spare parts inventory could be reduced saving capital, and repair work could be expedited with shop forces dealing with essentially the same problems regardless of locomotive type.

The on-line coal available in Montana, Roundup coal — a high grade lignite — was inferior in quality to the coal available in the Midwest, and required a locomotive with a large firebox in order to burn properly. The Northern Pacific used Rosebud coal, a lignite mined in Montana, and found that it required fireboxes with exceptionally large grate areas to provide enough air circulation to keep the coal burning hot enough to make steam. This in turn required locomotives with trailing trucks to support the weight of the large fireboxes.

The 2-6-2 Prairie was selected as one of the locomotive types to be used in dual service, mainly from Minneapolis to the Rocky Mountains and for freight service, the wide firebox type of 2-8-0 Consolidation would be used. The 4-6-2 Pacifics with different size wheels would be used for fast passenger service across the entire extension, and 2-8-2 Mikados (just coming into general useage) would be used for heavy freight service in the mountains. Helping the Mikados over the toughest grades was a job for the 2-6-6-2 compound Mallets, a recent development of heavy motive power that was finding wide favor on roads faced with long, steep mountain grades. The Great Northern was using them in the Cascades in 1906 as both road engines and pushers, and the Northern Pacific had ordered almost identical Belpaire boilered Mallets for use in both the Cascades and the Rockies.

The fast high stepping 4-4-2 Atlantic type was judged completely unsuitable for any type of service in the West, as they were having increasing difficulty handling heavy passenger trains even on the very flat grades in the Middle West.

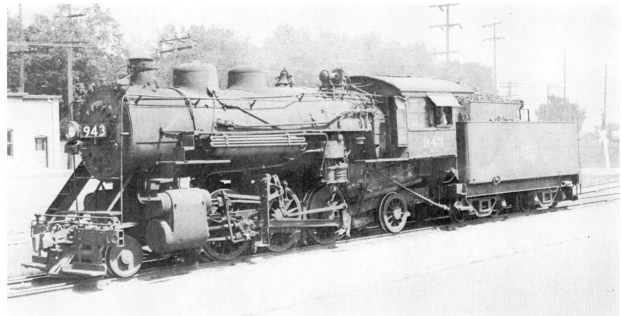

AT ONE TIME, A TOTAL of 195 Prairie types were in service between Minneapolis and the Pacific Coast. No. 924 was photographed at Othello, Washington, and 934 at Plymouth, Wisconsin in 1953.

Collection of Wally Swanson

Branch line power requirements of the Milwaukee would be filled by a potpourri of types, and the selection would be dictated as much by what was available from various motive power pools as by the service requirements. Ten Wheelers were regarded as unsuitable for main line use because of their lack of power, but the 4-6-0's, highly developed for dual service in the Midwest, were suitable for the light trackage of the western branches. Older and lighter Consolidations could also be used in the same type of service.

These were the general guidelines, initially established, and they would vary as the road gained experience in the West. Locomotives for construction work along the line were drawn from other parts of the railroad, the main consideration being that the types used would have to be light on their feet to avoid damaging new structures and roadbed. Old 4-4-0 American types, no longer suitable for main line use, were available in large numbers, and old Ten Wheelers were powerful enough to pull the construction outfits in the mountains. Simple very flexible narrow gauge tank type locomotives were used widely by contractors working on cuts, fills and in tunnels.

Prairies Class K

Built with large fireboxes to burn lignite, the short wheelbase Prairies, on 63" drivers, found immediate acceptance by the road when fifty were built in 1907 by the Brooks Works of American Locomotive Company. With a tractive effort of 33,320 lbs., they were less powerful than some of the early Consolidations, but could digest coal that gave other types of power severe indigestion.

Between 1907 and 1909, one hundred ninety-five of the type were built for the Milwaukee by Alco and the Milwaukee Shops. The Milwaukee and the Northern Pacific were among the largest users of the Prairie type, purchasing between them nearly a third of the fifteen hundred Prairies ever built. While other roads preferred Consolidations and Ten Wheelers, the Prairies did a fine job for the Milwaukee, doubling in freight and passenger service along the entire Pacific extension.

Originally intended as prairie power, they soon found their way onto every western division. Working in two's and three's, they could move considerable tonnage, even on the heavy mountain grades. Easy to fire, sturdy and reliable, they were, nevertheless as lignite burners, filthy engines to work on. Roundup and Rosebud coal were often referred to as "brown dirt" and at times was just about as flammable. When some of the class were converted to burn oil the Milwaukee firemen were envied by the firemen on the neighboring Northern Pacific, who were still stuck with hand firing their engines.

Consolidations Class C

The first Consolidation type locomotive to appear on the railroad was Class C1, built by Baldwin Locomotive Works in 1901. Four of the type were built, all with engine frames of forged iron, but two with wide fireboxes and a grate area of 46.5 sq. ft., and two with narrow fireboxes and a 35.1 sq. ft. grate area. Extensive testing proved the wide firebox to be the more efficient, and large numbers of them were built in the Milwaukee Shops, designated Class C1.

By 1910, new and heavier power was needed, and as part of the total number of new locomotives being built for western service, fifty new Consolidations Class C2 were ordered from Baldwin and twenty-five more were built by the railroad at Milwaukee. These 2-8-0's had larger cylinders than the Class C1 and the tractive effort was increased from 41,140 lbs. to 42,820 lbs.

In 1912, the railroad ordered the largest class of Consolidation yet built for the railroad, the Class C5. Fifty were constructed by American Locomotive and the Milwaukee Shops, and these engines while based on the earlier C2 design, were superheated, and the cylinders were increased to 24". The tractive effort was increased slightly to 43,130 lbs.

The C5's remained the largest 2-8-0's on the road until 1921, when the Chicago, Terre Haute & Southeastern Railroad was leased by the Milwaukee, and their Consolidations, which became Class C7, were acquired. Class C7, with a tractive effort of

PRAIRIE TYPE 5540 ON A WAY freight assignment, is tied up for the night at Neppel, Washington, in 1939. The ancient wooden caboose behind the engine is equipped with archbar trucks, long since outlawed by the ICC for interchange, but still allowed for light duty on a lightly travelled branch.

W. R. McGee

OLD OIL BURNING CONSOLIDATION Class C1c No. 1394, at Tacoma in 1956, was used mainly in the Tacoma yards. Although Tacoma was the western terminus of the electrification, all switching was done by steam power.

Collection of Wally Swanson

THE MOST POWERFUL CONSOLIDATIONS on the road, the Class C7 and C7a were acquired from the Chicago Terre Haute & South Eastern. Used mostly as heavy switchers and transfer locomotives, they put out almost 53,000 lbs. of tractive effort. No. 1357 is shown at Milwaukee.

Collection of Wally Swanson

CLASS C5a CONSOLIDATIONS, ON 63" drivers, had a tractive effort of 43,131 lbs. They ranged system wide as main line, branch and heavy switching power. No. 1239 is in Tacoma January, 1954, and No. 1274 is at Sioux City, Iowa.

Collection of Wally Swanson

AN OLD OIL BURNING HEAVY Consolidation type is pulling the new Olympian Hiawatha, complete with Fairbanks Morse diesels, backwards from Tacoma towards Union Station, Seattle in 1947. Overhead, the catenary stretches in a maze of intricate wire work.

Stuart Hertz

LOW WHEELED OIL BURNING Pacific No. 851 Class F5, at Othello, Washington in 1948, was built for mountain service. The 69" drivered 4-6-2's could exert a tractive effort of just over 43,000 lbs. and were the most powerful sub-class of Pacifics.

Collection of Wally Swanson

52,951 lbs. and 25" cylinders, then became the heaviest and most powerful class of Consolidation used by the railroad.

Although built in the early 1900's, many of the Consolidations remained in service well into the 1950's thanks to rebuilding programs that kept them serviceable. Many finished their careers as heavy switchers with modified clear vision tenders. Others were assigned to branches as helpers, and some performed heavy duty main line service, particularly during the war when anything that had wheels and a boiler was pressed into service. The oil burning type was popular with numerous branches in Washington state, and several were still in service in 1956.

Pacifics Class F

In 1905, when the last of the Atlantics was being built for the road, an experimental Pacific type, Class F2 was built in the Milwaukee Shops. Rather ungainly in appearance, it was almost identical to the Class G6 Ten Wheelers then being built, except that the boiler was lengthened and a pair of trailing wheels were located under the forward part of the cab. Potentially considerably more powerful than either the Atlantics or the Ten Wheelers, it was fitted with a very narrow firebox with only 35 sq. ft. of grate area mounted above the frame and behind the rear driver, that made it impossible to make the locomotive steam properly. As a result of

CLASS F3 PACIFIC NO. 6157 at Milwaukee was streamlined to become No. 151 Class F1 — Chippewa power.
Collection of Wally Swanson

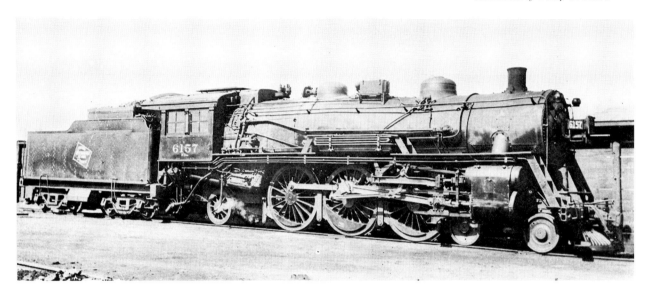

CLASS F3s PACIFIC NO. 167 at Madison, Wisconsin in 1954, and No. 163 at Milwaukee were built for service in the Midwest. They rolled on 79" drivers, and had a tractive effort of 31,873 lbs.

Collection of Wally Swanson

this difficulty, consideration of the Pacific type was dropped until 1910 when the Class F3, a new design by Alco, was introduced to the road.

The completion of the Pacific extension necessitated purchasing additional locomotives of all types, but it was obvious that the Atlantic type was too light for the heavier passenger equipment being put into service. The heavy grades and curvature of the new main line to the Pacific Coast, additionally complicated by bitter winter weather through the Dakotas and Montana that robbed much of the boiler heat through radiation, pulled the tractive effort of lighter passenger engines down to the point that double and triple heading would become a standard operation for hundreds of miles.

Seventy Class F3 locomotives were purchased from Alco and were immediately followed by twenty Class F4 locomotives built in the Milwaukee Shops. For all practical purposes, the F3 and F4 were identical, except that the Class F4, intended for service on the mountain divisions, had 69" rather than 79" drivers. The boilers of both classes were

identical to the boiler of the Class K1 Prairie type, and the grates were the same as those used on the L1 and L2 Class Mikados. Other parts were also interchangeable to simplify shop inventory and maintenance problems.

Late in 1910, the Class F5 Pacifics began to follow the F4's out of the Milwaukee Shops. Twenty were built between 1910 and 1912, and an additional fifty were received from Alco in 1912. Constructed for use on the Pacific extension, the Class F5 with 69" drivers, was very similar to the Class F4, but used superheated steam. When the electrification was completed, all of the F4's and F5's, except those needed between Avery and Othello, were moved back to the Middle West, and a number of them had extra tires shrunk over the driving wheels increasing their diameter to 73".

The Pacifics rendered long and valuable service to the road, and handled increasingly longer and heavier trains. Well built in the first place, they were modernized and rebuilt through the years to keep pace with the changing times. Four of the Pacifics —

94

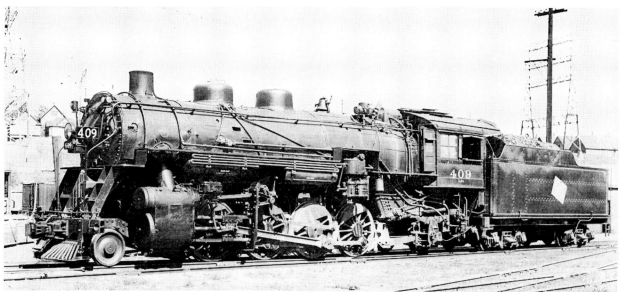

FOR YEARS, MIKADOS WERE the backbone of freight service on the Milwaukee. Class L2b, Nos. 400-499 was the biggest single sub-class, and when no longer suitable for main line service, some of the class became heavy switchers. No. 466 is in switching service at Minneapolis in 1954. No. 409 is in road service at St. Paul in 1957.

Collection of Wally Swanson

Mikados Class L

two F3's and two F5's — were put through a major rebuilding and modification program in the late 1930's and early 1940's to become streamlined power for the Chippewa and the Midwest Hiawatha. The F3's became Class F1 and the F5's became Class F2 with 73" drivers. The streamlined shrouds fitted to the engines made them, in some respects, look like a streamlined Hudson with a short tender. Overall the effect was impressive, and it was not apparent that a thirty year old locomotive was underneath all of the streamlining and new striped paint.

The most popular and widely used freight locomotive on the Milwaukee was the 2-8-2 Mikado. Northern Pacific had started the ball rolling in 1904, when the first of the very successful Class W Mikado type locomotives were built and put into service in the mountain districts. Other roads, noting the success of the type in heavy freight service, jumped on the bandwagon, and by the early 1920's, over ten thousand 2-8-2's were in service from coast to coast.

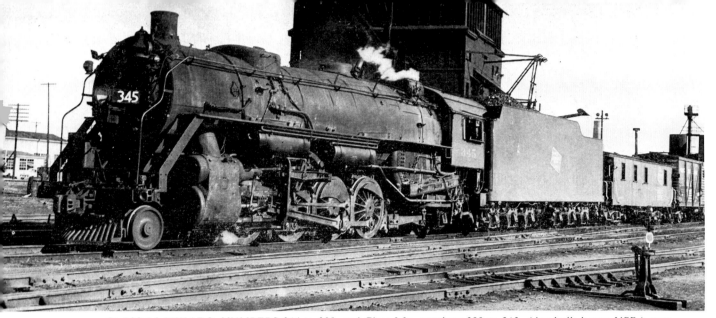

CLASS L3 MIKADO, NUMBERS 314 to 399, and Class L3a, numbers 300 to 313, Alco built heavy USRA type in 1918 and 1919, were the heaviest Mikes on the railroad, and with their increased capacity were very successful on the heavy tonnage districts, particularly between Minneapolis and Harlowton. 345 was photographed at Minneapolis in 1954.

Collection of Wally Swanson

Basically the Mikado was a simple engine to build, maintain and repair. Even a shop with limited facilities could do most of the repair work, which while heavy, was not complicated or sophisticated in nature. The firebox mounted above and behind the rear drivers (in most cases) allowed the 63" drivers to be fitted without raising the center line of the boiler to excessive heights to obtain driver clearance. Eight driving wheels and a trailing truck to support the firebox, kept the axle loading low so that the locomotive, particularly the lighter classes, was as much at home on the branch lines as on the main line. The large firebox meant that steaming qualities were good, and it was possible to keep the engine hot even while working hard. However, since most of the type were coal burning "hand bombers," they could work a single fireman to the point of exhaustion, and in heavy service two firemen working in relays were often used. Still the durability, power, speed capability and good steaming qualities of the Mikado, made them perhaps the best all around

freight power of the early Twentieth Century. During World War I, the United States Railway Administration standardized the Mikados into two classes — heavy and light — and thousands were built for the railroads up into the mid 1920's.

Twenty Class L1 Mikados, built by the Milwaukee Shops, entered service on the Pacific extension in 1909. With a tractive effort of 46,630 lbs. and on 63" drivers, the 260,000 lb. engines afforded relief to the hard working Prairies in service in the mountains and on the prairies. The company shops turned out forty more superheated Mikados, Class L2 in 1912, and one hundred forty more were built by Alco between 1912 and 1914.

In 1918-1919, one hundred heavy Mikados of USRA design were delivered to the road. The 320,000 lb. engines with bigger boilers and seventy square foot grates, but still on 63" drivers, had a tractive effort of just under 60,000 lbs. These engines were assigned systemwide. During 1920-1923, two hundred more Mikados Class L2b were delivered to

WEST OF LEWISTOWN, MONTANA, near Glengarry, a pair of Mikes, 626 and 651, muscle tonnage towards Judith Gap and Harlowton.

W. R. McGee

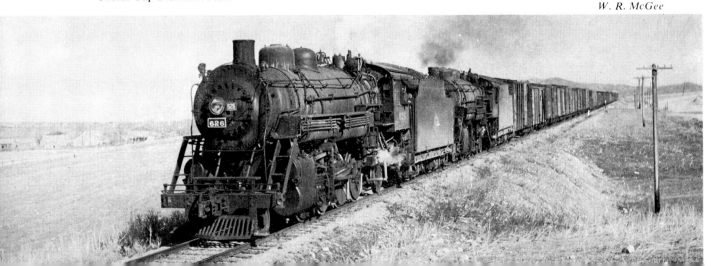

ORIGINALLY A CLASS N2 compound, built in 1911, Class N3 Mallet No. 65 at Tacoma in 1953, had been modernized along with sixteen others of the N2 Class (Nos. 50-66) in the 1930's, to increase the pulling power so that full trains could be handled over the freight line between Othello and Avery.

Collection of Wally Swanson

the road by Baldwin. They had the same 48.8 square foot grates of the early types that were interchangeable with those of the Prairies and Pacifics, but were heavier than the early models, delivering more tractive effort — 54,720 lbs. The early L1's were superheated and somewhat modernized, raising their tractive effort. By 1923, the Milwaukee had five hundred Mikados in service, riding turntables from Chicago to Tacoma, as the backbone of the steam freight power. Many of these Mikes outlasted newer and heavier steam power (suitable only for main line use) when diesel power took over during the 1950's.

Mallets Class N

Among the most interesting steam locomotives on the railroad were the Class N compound Mallets. There were two sub classes of the 2-6-6-2's, built by Alco, twenty-five Class N1's built in 1910 and 1911, and the eleven Class N2's built in 1912. The basic difference between the two classes was that the N1's used saturated steam, while the N2's were superheated. Both types were designed to haul nine hundred tons at six to eight miles per hour up a 2.7% grade — found on the west side of Snoqualmie Pass.

BY NO STRETCH OF THE IMAGINATION could the modernized old Mallets be called beautiful. No. 9314 (64) in Spokane in 1937, displays for all the world to see, the overhanging Coffin feedwater heater, peculiar headlight frame, and inside bearing trailing truck that all detracted from the appearance of the old engine. Capable, but slow, the main rods threatened to dig turf with every revolution of the 57" drivers.

W. R. McGee

Operation of the Class N locomotives in the Cascades was slow, but the 2-6-6-2's slogged their way up and down Snoqualmie Pass with little difficulty, other than a problem common to all Mallets, they couldn't seem to pass a water plug and refueling also was constantly necessary. Seventeen of the locomotives were coal burners, and the remaining eight, operating in the Idaho Forest Reserve, burned oil to lessen fire danger from burning cinders.

The real trouble with the Mallets began in Montana, where at times in the sub-zero weather, the road was threatened with a complete tie-up. The trouble stemmed mainly from the very flexible live steam and exhaust connections between the high and low pressure cylinders. All of these connections leaked steam badly, an irritation or nuisance in the rather mild climate of the Cascades, but a serious problem in the bitter climate of Idaho and Montana where it condensed onto the railhead freezing the drivers to the rail. More power then had to be called to push the stalled locomotive and its train into motion — if possible.

The large exposed steam lines also radiated much needed heat into the frigid atmosphere. While cold weather affected the performance of all steam locomotives to some degree, reducing tonnage by 25 to 30%, the Mallets were so adversely affected that they were rated unsatisfactory by the Milwaukee for the main line service that they had been designed for. With the completion of the electrification on the Rocky Mountain and Coast Divisions, the Mallets were assigned to the Idaho Division (running between Avery and Othello), to logging or branch lines in Washington and Idaho, and to the old Tacoma & Eastern operating out of Tacoma. On the Idaho Division, the ruling grade eastbound was .4% and westbound it was 1%. Here again the Mallets fell down as they could not handle full tonnage brought into Avery and Othello by the electrics. The Mallets needed steam even going down the 1% grade.

With an expensive electrification program just completed, that still had to be paid for, the road was not in a position to buy new locomotives to pull heavy tonnage across the two hundred twenty-five mile gap in the electrification between Avery and Othello, yet with the steam power available the gap was a bottleneck. An engineering study was made to determine just what could be done with the Mallets, the heaviest and potentially most powerful steam locomotive that the road owned. The completed study indicated that if the locomotives were rebuilt as simple engines, and if the evaporative capacity of the boiler were increased, the locomotives could handle five thousand tons eastbound over the .4% grades of the freight line via Malden on the Idaho Division.

One engine was rebuilt, and when tests indicated a successful solution to the problem, sixteen more of the Mallets were rebuilt. Tractive effort was increased from 70,440 lbs. to 82,720 lbs., and at fifteen miles per hour, 67,000 lbs. of tractive effort was still being produced. Superheater and Coffin feedwater heaters were applied, new front frames and cylinders were constructed, and the live steam exhaust piping and flexible connections were rebuilt to solve the leakage problems. Boiler tube pilots replaced the old wooden pilots, and the headlight was lowered to the pilot deck to improve lighting of the track on curves. New all welded six wheel truck, high capacity tenders were built in the Milwaukee Shops. All of the changes, including the new smaller front cylinders, improved the appearance of the locomotives, and a new paint scheme that included striping on the tenders and large colorful heralds on the flanks of the tender, contributed to a more modern appearance.

Driver size remained at 57", and the rods still threatened to cut wayside grass with every revolution of the drivers. Nevertheless, the seventeen rebuilt and modernized locomotives, now classed as N3's, could now get across the Idaho Division with five thousand tons. Speed capacity was still low, but the performance was so improved, that purchasing of new locomotives was forestalled until after World War II, when the Mallets were among the first locomotives scrapped as newer power became available.

SWEAT OUTLINES water compartments on the tank of Mike 392, as it pounds out of Minneapolis on a blistering day in August, 1954. The 8,000 gallon welded tank of a scrapped Mallet behind it, adds considerable bulk to the already large USRA type Mike.

Jack Malven

TEN WHEELERS WERE HIGHLY REGARDED BY THE MILWAUKEE AS dual service power for years throughout the Midwest. After completion of the Pacific extension in 1909, a number of them were transferred to the West as branch line power. No. 1072 Class G7c is at Three Forks, Montana in 1956, and No. 1173 Class G6 is at Marquette, Iowa in 1953.

Collection of Wally Swanson

Ten Wheelers Class G

The road had started using 4-6-0's in 1881, when thirty were purchased for freight service from the Rhode Island Locomotive Works. The great bulk of the ten wheel type locomotive, however, were built between 1892 and 1901. Most of these were Baldwin Vauclain compounds — small high pressure cylinders on top of the large low pressure cylinders driving the same rod. Large numbers of these locomotives were rebuilt to single expansion, and survived as Class G5 through G8 into the 1950's.

Popular on the Milwaukee Road, the Ten Wheelers were excellent dual service engines, fast for freight service and capable for passenger service. Some of the later types could turn a fast wheel while developing over 36,000 lbs. of tractive effort. They were often the only type of power on branch lines with a light enough axle loading to cross the light bridges and trestles and to be easy on the light rail.

The Ten Wheelers could also make fairly good speed on tight curves and through short radius switches due to the better guiding qualities of the four wheel lead truck.

Some of the early Ten Wheelers were among the first locomotives on the road to feature a wide rather than a long and narrow firebox. The long narrow firebox had grown to ten feet in length, about the practical limit for a hand fired locomotive. In experiments with some of the 4-6-0's the firebox was widened to create sufficient grate area to make the locomotive steam well, and the results of these experiments led directly to the adoption of the wide firebox.

Over one hundred twenty of the type were still in service as late as World War II, and two 69" wheeled 4-6-0's (Nos. 10 and 11) were rebuilt for the North Woods Hiawatha service. The various rebuilding programs made some of the locomotives look quite modern, although the tall shotgun stacks and huge domes still served to date them as turn of the century locomotives.

99

CLASS A4as ATLANTIC NO. 3135, in commuter service in 1939, was one of few converted to burn oil in the Midwest. The tall 79" drivers and 200 lbs. boiler pressure did not allow much tractive effort, but once rolling, they were fully capable of speeds in the high 80's.

Collection of Wally Swanson

Atlantics Class A

If the Bi-polar electric locomotive was the flag bearer of the Milwaukee in transcontinental service, then certainly it was the Atlantic "Hiawatha" type of steam locomotive that was the flag bearer of the Milwaukee in the hotly competitive passenger traffic of the Middle West. It was the streamlined 4-4-2 Class A locomotive, coupled to new light-weight "conventional" equipment that kept the image of the Milwaukee bright and shining in an era when the streamlined diesels and articulated equipment, particularly of the Burlington and the Union Pacific, threatened to capture the fancy and cash of the traveling public in the mid 1930's.

For a number of reasons, the Milwaukee had opted not to build or have built a diesel powered articulated streamliner similar to the early Zephyr or City streamliners. Articulated streamliners were, in essence, "unit" trains that lacked flexibility in the make-up of the consist, and turning an entire train intact at terminals presented problems. At this date — 1935 — diesel power was far more costly than steam power, and had not conclusively proven itself. The Milwaukee was not yet prepared to streamline the Olympian or its other intercity passenger equipment, and the Milwaukee Shops were not in a position to tool up and build equipment that could not be used system wide.

Other than the initial cost of diesels, there were other valid reasons why the Milwaukee chose steam to power the new Hiawatha streamliners. Existing facilities could be utilized to service and shop steam locomotives. The position of the crew in a cab at the back of the locomotive was safer, in event of a grade crossing accident, than it would be sitting in a cab mounted over the lead truck. Most important, the

terrain over which the new Hiawathas would be traveling between Chicago and Twin Cities, was eminently suited to the high speed capabilities of steam power. With grades and curvature between the terminals, for all practical purposes, negligible, a high speed steam engine of simple basic design could be built to take full advantage of the flat terrain, with no need to compromise the speed capability for grades or curves.

American Locomotive Company was chosen as the builder, and industrial designer, Otto Kuhler, was placed in charge of the styling and streamlining. The locomotive selected, the 4-4-2 Atlantic, holder of many speed records, was no stranger to the Milwaukee Road. The design dated back to the 1890's, when their service on other roads had demonstrated a remarkable ability to make time even with a heavy train. In 1896, two Vauclain compounds were delivered to the road by Baldwin Locomotive Works. They were among the first locomotives to combine excellent high speed characteristics with a good tractive effort through the use of a large capacity boiler that developed high horsepower at speed.

In 1897, one of the type, No. 839 (with 78" drivers), pulling a thirteen car train, made a record run between Forest Glen and Milwaukee — seventy-four miles in eighty-two minutes — and promptly became embroiled in a controversy when the results of this run were published, and the article appeared in England. The *Engineer* in London questioned the design of the locomotive, and broadly hinted at the validity of the record run. Mr. S. M. Vauclain, the General Manager of Baldwin, replied to these charges in *Railroad Gazette,* and verified the accuracy of the timing of the record run and vouched for the capability of the locomotive in Milwaukee Road service. A few years after this transatlantic debate, the Atlantic type was introduced in England, subsequently became widely used, and established more records in fast passenger service. Eleven more were put into service on the Milwaukee before the turn of the century, and additional classes of Atlantics were delivered through January, 1909, concluding with the balanced compounds (high pressure cylinders inside the frame and low pressure cylinders outside the frame). These had 85" drivers, the tallest driver ever used on a Milwaukee locomotive.

As trains became heavier, the design fell into disfavor, as locomotive weight on the drivers particularly, could not be increased to gain more tractive effort, because the rail, bridge structures and roadbed would not take the increased axle loading. However, some of the early Class A's were converted to single expansion with driver size reduced to 79", and were used into the 1940's.

The four Class A locomotives of 1935, 1936 and 1937, built to power the Hiawathas, were undoubtedly the most famous Atlantics ever built. Under their handsome and colorful streamlined shrouds — regarded by many as the most beautiful streamlining ever given a steam locomotive — these locomotives were as different from the early Class A's, as the Ford Trimotor was from the DC-6.

While both classes of Atlantics could run constantly at speeds of over ninety miles per hour, the designed speed of the streamlined A's was listed at over one hundred miles per hour. The tractive effort of the 1935 version of the 4-4-2 was nearly 31,000 lbs., almost half again as much as the 22,000 lbs. tractive effort of the early versions. The weight of the locomotive was increased from 108,000 lbs. to 144,000 lbs., and the boiler pressure was raised from 200 to 300 lbs. The boilers of the streamliners, which burned oil, were made of high tensile steel, and a superheater raised the steam temperature to 750 degrees at the cylinders.

Every modern appliance known to further reliability and ease of maintenance and operation was applied. Both the engine and the tender were equipped with roller bearings, and drivers selected were of the Boxpok design. Driving rods were made of alloy steel, light yet strong and simpler to counterbalance. The engine frame, cylinders, frame supports, appliance mountings and even the air reservoirs were cast as a complete unit, eliminating hundreds of bolts and nuts and the problem of continual maintenance. Water capacity was 13,000 gallons. Pressure alemite lubrication was used so that no greasing or oiling would be necessary between terminals, and the all welded tender carried 4,000 gallons of oil so that it would not be necessary to refuel between terminals.

A notable first scored by the 1935-1937 Atlantics was that the streamlined shroud was not merely an attempt to disguise an old engine, but was designed as a part of the locomotive. The clasp brakes — a brake shoe on each side of the wheel — fitted to every wheel on the locomotive and tender for maximum braking power, was another first. With all of these features, the four streamlined Class A's cost only about as much as one diesel. With hundreds of thousands of high speed miles beneath their wheels, and having established numerous speed records, they were retired from service in the 1950's.

HUDSON 132, AFTER BRINGING THE eastbound Columbian into Avery from Spokane, has been cut off and released via the main line crossover in front of E-14. To the far left a four unit diesel with a westbound freight waits for the Columbian to pull out, and a four unit electric freight motor waits to help an eastbound freight due momentarily in Avery.

Philip C. Johnson

HIAWATHA CLASS A No. 3, at Milwaukee in June, 1940, is being readied for an outbound trip. In line, color and overall appearance, the Class A's were among the most beautiful locomotives ever operated in the United States, rivalled only by the handsome Daylights on the Southern Pacific. The streamlined Hudsons, Class F-7, were magnificent, but lacking the clean simple streamlining of the A's, tended to look "overdressed."

Collection of Roger Lins

Hudsons Class F

Since 1925, the Milwaukee had pioneered research on a 4-6-4 type for heavy passenger service, but lacked the funds to have one built for test purposes. In 1929, with the financial condition of the road somewhat improved, fourteen 4-6-4's were delivered to the road by Baldwin Locomotive Works. Thirteen of them were put into service immediately between Minneapolis and Chicago, running between these two terminals without change. The fourteenth Hudson, along with the first 4-8-4 delivered to the road, were put into test service between Minneapolis and Harlowton, a through run of nine hundred fourteen miles. This run very nearly equalled the Northern Pacific run of one thousand eight miles between Minneapolis and Livingston, using Class A Northerns.

The sustained high horsepower characteristics of the big Hudsons at speed was a significant improvement over the older and smaller Pacifics that lacked the capability of keeping increasingly heavy trains to a fast schedule. Starting tractive effort of the Hudsons was not much greater than that of the Pacifics, 45,820 lbs. to 43,120 lbs., but the tractive effort of the Pacifics dropped off rapidly in the higher speed ranges with a heavy train. On the other hand, roller bearings on lead and trailing trucks, the big boilers and the large stoker fed fireboxes of the Hudsons, all contributed to high speed performance with heavy trains. The Hudson type was quick to demonstrate on the Milwaukee what had been learned on the New York Central — that they were without peer in heavy passenger service operating on a water level route.

On the negative side, Hudsons tended to be very slippery when starting a heavy train, and required careful handling. Some of the machinery, particularly the main pins, tended to run hot during sustained high speed operations, and the cab pitched and bounced hard at high speeds. Also the stoker screw jammed easily if a foreign object got mixed in with the coal and entered the stoker mechanism, but overall the Hudsons were remarkable engines and established many records in sustained high speed operation.

The fastest track between Minneapolis and the Coast lies in the rolling prairie country between Minneapolis and Harlowton. The curves are wide and the grades are light, with only one stretch of 1% grade eastbound out of Marmarth, North Dakota. Grades westbound do not exceed .6%. The Olympian and Columbian, trains 15/16 and 17/18, powered by Class F3 and F5 Pacifics, made seven engine changes between Minneapolis and Harlowton. With ten minutes allowed for each change of power, over an hour could be eliminated from the schedule if the engine changing could be eliminated. The power requirements of the Olympian which averaged eight hundred trailing tons, and the topography seemed well suited to the operating characteristics of the big Hudsons, and testing revealed that the Class F6 Hudsons could handle this train without a change of power. A full take over by the Hudsons awaited only the delivery of more of the type to the road. Eight more Class F6a Hudsons were purchased in the early 1930's. The Milwaukee was the only one of the three Northwest carriers to purchase Hudsons. The Great Northern used Mountains and Northerns on the Empire Builder and Oriental Limited, and the Northern Pacific used only the Northern on their North Coast Limited.

Perhaps the most difficult service that the Hudsons were called upon to perform was on the head end of the Olympian during World War II. This transcontinental was running filled to capacity, often in two sections, heavy with extra head end cars and troop Pullmans. Normal train length prior to the war was eight to ten cars. This was stretched to as many as seventeen cars on occasion, and twelve to fifteen cars was common. All of the equipment, except for a lightweight coach and possibly a dining car, were heavyweight, made up of extra elderly coaches and head end cars with old brass journals that increased starting and rolling resistance. Literally everything that would still roll was pressed into service. Coming east, the trains were often several hours late into Harlowton, and as the big electrics silently pulled away, a hot and smoking F6 would lock couplers with the first car. A quick check of the train, a high-ball signal from the rear end, and in the cab, air was released as the throttle came back. High 79" drivers bit into sanded rail, and with a sharp barking exhaust that rattled nearby windows, train 16 would get underway again. With the heavy wartime loads, it was nearly impossible to make up time, but the remarkable thing is that no further time was usually lost on the nearly one thousand miles into Minneapolis.

In 1944, the power short Idaho Division received help in the form of two modified oil burning Hudsons Class F6a to work the Olympian. The Hudson type west of Minneapolis was not a novelty on other roads,

notably the Santa Fe from Chicago to LaJunta, Colorado and the Canadian Pacific with Hudsons in dual service as far west as Calgary, Alberta. However a Hudson type in the Pacific Northwest was about as common as an Atlantic in freight service. The Idaho Division included some fast track west of Marengo to Othello, but eastbound out of Spokane to Manito, a sharp grade and heavy curvature made a helper necessary if the train was heavy, even when the 4-8-4's were on the Point. The two oil burning F6a's were used right up into the 1950's on the head end of the streamlined Olympian Hiawatha and Columbian, and alternated in this service with a pair of Class S1 oil burning Northerns. Actually many of the design features of the F6 and S1 classes, both Baldwin built, were remarkably similar with interchangeable parts, and the two were very much at home operating out of the same terminals.

In the Middle West the success story of the Hudsons in Hiawatha service is well known. The modern streamlined 84" drivered Class F7's, delivered to the road in late 1938, performed remarkable feats on the racetrack between Minneapolis and Chicago. On the Milwaukee to Chicago multiple track main line, speeds in the high 90's and over 100 mph was a common everyday occurrence. Delivery of the F7's from American Locomotive Works released the earlier model F6's to work the Minneapolis Harlowton main line, but so far as can be determined from locomotive assignment records, no streamlined F7 was ever assigned to work west of Minneapolis on a regularly scheduled basis.

HUDSON 105 BEGINS to move out of Minneapolis with the Morning Hiawatha to Chicago. As the 84" drivers begin to turn, a feather of white steam blows back from the steam generator, and the fireman leans far out of the cab.
Don Dietrich

WITH SMOKEBOX MOUNTED BELL clanging its warning, Hudson No. 131 backs down the main line in Othello to pick up the eastbound Olympian Hiawatha for the run into Spokane. The big 79" drivered 4-6-4, although not suited for service on the heavy mountain grades, was fully capable of keeping the Olympian Hiawatha to time on the fast track between Othello and Avery.

Collection of Wally Swanson

CLASS F6a HUDSON NO. 146 at Deerfield, Illinois in 1953, features a modified front end that looks like a plumber's bad dream. Very fast and capable, the unstreamlined Milwaukee Hudsons lacked the classic simple lines of the New York Central Hudsons.

Collection of Wally Swanson

Northerns Class S

In 1929, the road received its first Class S1 Northern 4-8-4 type from Baldwin. Except for a longer wheel base to mount eight 74" drivers and a larger firebox, it was almost identical in appearance to the Class F6 Hudson. The F6 and S1 Classes were designed to incorporate as many interchangeable parts as possible, and this accounted for the striking similarity in appearance, even to the "rollerskate" outside bearing lead truck. Far and away the largest steam engine on the road, the locomotive, with tender, weighed nearly three quarters of a million pounds. Starting tractive effort (62,130 lbs.) was less than that of the modernized Mallets, but the 4-8-4 could sustain this effort in speed ranges that were so far beyond the speed capabilities of the low wheeled Mallets, there really was no comparison in performance.

The first locomotive No. 9700, was followed several years later by a companion engine, and in the general re-numbering of all locomotives in 1938, 9700 became No. 250, and the second engine retained its original No. 251. Both locomotives were converted to burn oil, and assigned to the Idaho Division in the 1930's, due to a critical shortage of modern steam power in this area. The Northerns, the only modern heavy dual service steam engines on the road, were warmly welcomed by the engine crews and operating officials of the Idaho Division, particularly in passenger service. The track between Avery and Marengo was fast track, and the S1's could keep to a schedule, making up time if necessary. The numerous tight curves and short stiff grades from Marengo into Spokane sapped the power of the old Pacifics so that doubleheading was often necessary. Another stiff grade out of Spokane to Manito and Plummer Junction hampered the older power, and here too, the S1's could usually lift a heavy train out of the Spokane River Valley in a solo effort. Cost conscious officials welcomed the elimination of the usual helper crew, and the savings in fuel and time. Harried conductors, used to making out delay reports, praised the capabilities and capacity of the big Northerns. Engine crews welcomed the higher pay scale and safer operation, as well as the comparatively easy riding made possible by eliminating another engine pounding along behind.

ON SEPTEMBER 2, 1950 IN AVERY, Idaho — the west end of the Bitter Root Range electrification — Hudsons 131 and 132, and Northern 251 wait to take over the evening's westbound Olympian Hiawatha and Columbian. In the engine shed, boxcab motor E-34 and a Little Joe wait to be called for eastbound tonnage.

Dr. Philip R. Hastings

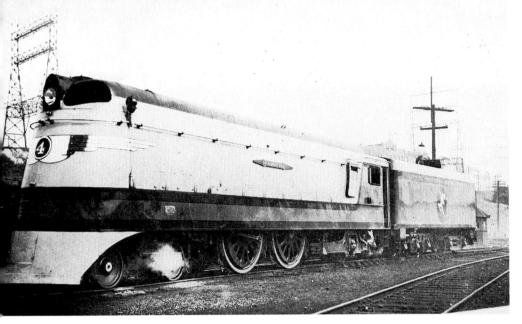

CLASS A ATLANTIC No. 4 waits at Milwaukee in 1938. The streamlined Atlantics, uncommonly beautiful in their orange, silver and maroon color scheme, were regarded by many as the epitomy of streamlined steam power.
Collection of Wally Swanson

In November, 1937, the thirty 4-8-4 locomotives (No. 200-229) Class S2 began arriving on the road. Built by Baldwin, the roller bearing equipped engines retained the 74" drivers of the earlier class, but the boiler pressure was up from 225 to 285 lbs., tractive effort was increased to 70,800 lbs. and the locomotive and tender weight was increased to 887,450 lbs. The big Northerns were primarily intended for freight service, but could double in passenger service. Equipped with vestibule cabs and huge all-welded tanks, they were handsome locomotives, and their service capability had been long awaited by the operating department, as a replacement for many of the smaller Mikes. All were assigned east of the Rocky Mountains.

In 1944, the Milwaukee was critically short of modern heavy power, and every locomotive that could still turn a wheel had long since been pressed into service to cope with the rising wartime tonnage. The road would have preferred diesels for freight service, but was allocated ten 4-8-4 locomotives (No. 260-269) Class S3, built by Alco. A composite design, built with substitute non-critical materials in some instances, they were only about as powerful as the early S1, although considerably heavier. Four of the class, converted to oil, were sent west to work on the Idaho Division for use in both freight and passenger service. Stark in appearance, they performed well, until, caught in the overwhelming flood of more efficient diesel power, they were scrapped in the 1950's.

EF1 Freight Motors

When the Milwaukee Road made the decision in 1914 to electrify the railroad from Harlowton, Montana to Avery, Idaho — a distance of 440 miles — an order for electric locomotives was placed with American Locomotive Company-General Electric

Manufacturing Company for a total of 84 units, with delivery to be completed by late 1916. These 84 units were actually 42 two-unit semi-permanently coupled locomotives or motors, comprising 12 passenger and 30 freight locomotives. All 84 units, at this time, were built with complete cabs so that they could be operated bi-directionally as two unit locomotives, or singly in local freight or passenger service. Some of the freight "singles" survived into the 1960's.

The first locomotive to arrive on the railroad, in September, 1915, was locomotive No. 10200, consisting of an A and a B unit, with a 2-B-B/B-B-2 wheel arrangement. One hundred twelve feet long, the 288 ton monster was the largest electric locomotive in the world, and the pride of the railroad. Capable of pulling a 2,600 ton train up a 1% grade at 16 mph., the eight motors gave the huge locomotive a total of 3,440 hp. on a continuous rating, or 4,110 hp. for one hour. Starting tractive effort was rated as high as 146,000 lbs. or as low as 112,000 lbs. depending on the condition of the rail. This much effort could be exerted only for a relatively short time, and the continuous tractive effort rating at 16 mph. was 70,700 lbs. Nevertheless, this "giant of the rails" was nearly as powerful as three Mikado (2-8-2) steam engines, and the railroad ordered the electric locomotives to replace steam with this ratio in mind. Not only were the locomotives of the EF1 class the largest electric locomotives in the world, they were also the first direct current locomotives ever built to operate at a potential as high as 3,000 volts (later increased to 3,400 volts).

They were also the first to employ direct current regenerative braking. Regenerative braking was little understood except by the electrical engineers who designed the system and one of the best explanations, in layman's language, of how it worked is to be found in the May 1916 issue of the employees' magazine, *Milwaukee Railway System*. "Regenerative braking is a process of producing electrical current within the motors of the locomotive by converting the motors into generators, and the current thus produced being returned to the trolley; and the force of gravity which tends to make the train run away down grade is the power that drives the generators, and the work thus performed operates to hold the train back. Through the line current control this retardation is controlled by the engineer who thus handles the speed of the train as his judgement suggests."

There were times when the electrification was new, primarily due to lack of experience, that the judgement of the engineer was not too good in handling the regenerative braking, and using the air brakes to maintain control while switching into regenerative braking. Since switching into regenerative braking was nearly impossible beyond speeds of seventeen miles per hour in parallel operation, or eight miles per hour in series operation, when descending a grade, air brake control had to be maintained until the regenerative braking began to take effect or a heavy train could accelerate too rapidly. Attempting to go into regenerative braking at too great a speed would result in the circuit breakers blowing, and it was impossible to go into regenerative braking until the speed came down again. The locomotive had to be eased into regenerative, not unlike a heavy truck shifting down through gears to maintain control. Missing a shift in a heavily loaded truck on a steep grade results in a runaway, and missing the regenerative point in an electric locomotive, without proper air brake control, had the same result — a runaway. Properly used, however, the regenerative braking was a godsend to train operation on the long and steep mountain grades.

Once in regenerative almost any speed desired could be maintained without ever touching the air brakes, and the air brakes were only needed for stopping. The motors were now, in fact, generators or producers of power, rather than consumers, and power was being returned to the trolley and thence to the powerhouse or to trains needing power on the other side of the mountain. As much as 50% of the power used in coming up the grade could now be returned. The considerable saving in wear and tear on airbrake systems, wheels and brake shoes was an important contribution as these items comprised a large share of operating expense in mountain districts.

The new electric locomotives were welcomed by officials of the railroad, and the public during an exhibition tour which included the cities of Chicago, Milwaukee, Minneapolis/St. Paul and several smaller cities, before entering service in late 1915. The new features were welcomed by the engine crews too. The simple operation, easy riding, good visibility, elimination of smoke in the tunnels, cab heaters and insulated cabs were among the many improvements over the old steamers. Commenting on Mallet steam operation in the bitter winter cold of Montana, one operating official remarked, "All they ever did was leak steam and freeze up." The new electrics quickly demonstrated their worth when two of them hauled a 3,000 ton train up the 1.66% grade between Deer Lodge and Three Forks at 16 mph. A trio of steamers (two L class Mikes and a Mallet pusher) with 2,000 tons on the same grade could make just over half that speed — 9 mph.

WITH A BIG HUDSON on the point, the Morning Hiawatha accelerates out of Union Depot in St. Paul in May, 1940. Put into service in 1935, between the Twin Cities and Chicago, the Hiawathas were an immediate success with the traveling public.

W. R. McGee

PHOTOGRAPHED BY WARREN McGee in Spokane in 1937, Baldwin built No. 9700 (250), on the point of the Olympian, was the first Class S1 Northern delivered to the road in 1929. A companion locomotive No. 251 joined No. 9700 several years later.

In the 1920's and 1930's, with the advent of stronger draft gear in freight equipment generally, some of the original units were modified by removal of their lead wheels and operating compartments, and became essentially booster units, so that complete locomotives could be made up of one to four units with a cab on one or both ends of the locomotive as operating flexibility required. The arrangement was almost identical to that used in assembling many diesel units into one locomotive with cab or booster units as needed.

In heavy service since 1915 in the five mountain ranges between Harlowton and Tacoma, the big electric freight motors have paid back, many times over, the original cost of approximately $300,000 per locomotive. What other railroad can claim that motive power purchased fifty-five years ago is still in heavy main line service?

Class EP1

In 1916, the first electric passenger motors, Class EP1 entered service on the Milwaukee Road. The Class EP1 locomotives differed from the Class EF1 locomotives only in their gear ratio, train heating boiler, water and oil tanks, and a motor generator set for car lighting, which made them about thirty-three tons heavier than the freight motors. The passenger motors were geared for a 60 mph. top speed — the freight motors were geared for 45 mph. maximum speed. Horsepower developed was identical, except that the passenger motors developed their continuous horsepower rating at 29 mph. and the freight motors developed theirs at about 15.5 mph. In other words, the freight motors could grind upgrade with a long heavy freight drag — the passenger motors required a lighter train, but moved it twice as fast.

The running gear was designed to take all loads, while the boxcab bodies were flexibly mounted on the articulated running gear by center pin outside bearing mountings. Driving wheels were 52" diameter and the leading wheels were 36" diameter. Each driving axle was powered by a single 1,500 volt motor, two of which were connected in series to take the 3,000 volt trolley pressure.

The mechanical construction of electric locomotives is to a large degree determined by the type of

A FAMILIAR SIGHT ON THE water level grades of the east, and the Chicago-Minneapolis racetrack of the Milwaukee Road, Hudson Number 132 seems out of its element as it drifts downgrade with the Columbian, into the Spokane River Valley on Union Pacific track, in August, 1950.

Dr. Philip R. Hastings

BALDWIN BUILT IN 1930, Class S1 Northern type 250 and 251 were converted to oil burners and assigned to dual service between Othello and Avery, Idaho in the late 1930's. Due to the modified front ends with lowered headlight, and "roller skate" type of lead truck, also used on some of the early Hudson types, they were probably the most distinctive in appearance of the three classes of 4-8-4's.

Photographed by W. R. McGee at Othello May, 1950

motors used, the type of drive, and by the requirements for double-end operation. The oldest form of drive and one which is still used, is the axle mounted motor driving through single gear reduction.

On the Class EP1 and EF1 series, the motor is supported by the truck axle, which passed through bearings on the motor frame. A sprung projection on the frame, called the nose, rests on the truck bolster, supporting the other side of the motor. About 50% of the weight of the motor is thereby carried directly on the axle without spring support. A pinion (gear) on each end of the armature shaft engages a large gear, spring loaded, on the axle inside the driving wheel. The speed of rotation of the armature exceeds that of the wheel by the ratio of gear teeth to pinion teeth, 18:28 on the EP1's and 29:17 on the EF1's.

The driving torque was transmitted from the large gear to the driving wheel through short coil springs interposed between the gear rack and the gear center, the latter being rigidly keyed to the axle. This very flexible arrangement (not to be confused with quill drive) was thought necessary to protect the gears from wear and the shock of slipping or starting heavy trains. Service use after a number of years though, showed undue maintenance was required, and the spring loaded gears were consequently replaced with solid gears.

Like the freight motors, the passenger versions were two unit, semi-permanently coupled locomotives of 2-B-B/B-B-2 wheel arrangement, and could be separated for single unit operation, as some were for local passenger service. There was actually a total of twenty-four units in passenger service, making up twelve articulated locomotives. These twelve locomotives were powerful, having a continuous tractive effort rating of 43,000 lbs., a one hour rating of 60,000 lbs., and a maximum tractive effort at 25% adhesion of 122,000 lbs. Horsepower developed at the continuous rating was 3,340 hp., while at the one hour rating the horsepower increased to 4,100. The one unit rating — for those used in local passenger service was of course, 50% of the above figures, and a single unit weighed 321,000 lbs. with 244,000 lbs. on the drivers.

It is interesting to note that the later passenger locomotives, the EP2 and EP3 classes, which replaced the EP1's in 1920, exceeded these impressive ratings by very little. As a matter of fact the EP1 locomotives could do 70 mph. while the EP3 class was rated at 65 mph. Converted back to their original design as freight motors in 1920, and out of passenger service until 1953, five of the units were reconverted as passenger motors to power the Olympian Hiawatha on the Coast Division and Rocky Mountain Division, a fitting tribute to the excellent performance of these nearly forty year old locomotives.

Class EF2, EF3 and EF5 Freight Motors

By 1949, with twelve of the original freight units converted to cabless boosters, the classification of the freight motors was changed to differentiate between the various combinations available for freight service. Two unit motors with cabs were classified as EF1. Three unit motors with cabs were classified as EF2. EF3 motors were three units with the center

unit a cabless booster. EF5 motors were composed of four units, either all cab units or two cab and two booster units.

The cabless booster units were reduced in overall length from 56' to 41'6", and the wheelbase, with the removal of the lead truck, was reduced from 45' 10" to 32'. The modifications, very slightly, increased the tractive effort since all the weight was now concentrated on the drivers. A four unit locomotive, with two booster units, was reduced in length by nearly thirty feet, improving the handling, particularly in terminal areas.

The main advantage gained was in the simplification of controls and in reduced maintenance. Some combinations were designed to be operated primarily from one end, but retained the capability of control from either end. Helper locomotives, mostly four unit combinations, had identical controls at either end, and control could be changed from one end to the other. Thus a helper, at the top of a mountain grade, could run light back down grade, with control now in what had been the trailing unit.

Class ES2, Switchers

Other than the "Little Joes," the only electric locomotives to be bought "off the shelf" by the Milwaukee Road, were the Class ES2 seventy ton switchers. Two were purchased in 1916 and two more in 1919. The four locomotives were identical except that the last two purchased in 1919 were about twelve tons heavier than their predecessors.

Built by Alco-GE, the little 70 and 82 ton steeple cab locomotives had a B-B wheel arrangement with each of the four axles powered by a

NORTHERN 251, recently shopped, backs down the main in Othello to pick up the eastbound Columbian running late because of snow in the mountains.

Don Dietrich

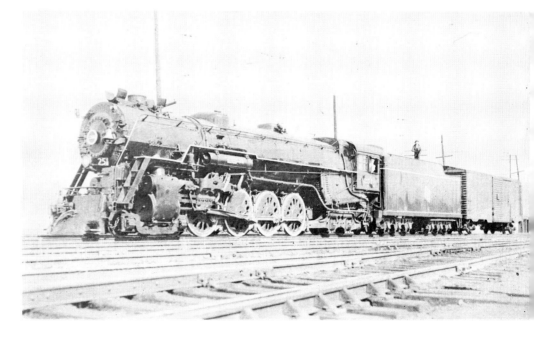

111

BALDWIN BUILT CLASS S2 Northern type, numbers 201 to 240, comprising the most numerous and most powerful class of 4-8-4's on the railroad, were used largely in freight service. All had vestibule cabs, peculiar sounding air horns, and the off center smokebox front mounted bell. Some were equipped with Mars lights, and stack extensions were used on a few of the type, as on 217. Due to wartime power shortages, some of the class worked as far west as Othello. Burning coal, they were restricted from working in Idaho because of the increased fire danger to forests. 221 and 239 were photographed at St. Paul and 217 at Othello.

Collection of Wally Swanson

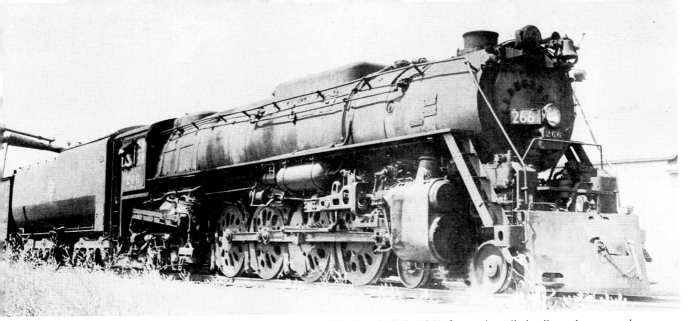

CLASS S3 NORTHERN TYPE, Numbers 260 to 269, Alco built in 1944, featured vestibule all weather type cabs, and a modified Vanderbilt water bottom tender. Due to the use of a single steam and sand dome housing, and a lagged smokebox with very little piping exposed, the clean, uncluttered outline of the S3's resembled, in some respects, the Niagara type 4-8-4 on the New York Central. Four of the class, 262, 263, 267 and 269, were converted to oil and used between Othello and Avery in dual service. Engine 266 was photographed at Milwaukee.

Collection of Wally Swanson

geared swivel truck GE 255A series motor. Unlike all other Milwaukee Road motors, the switcher was designed to take all tractive loads through the body frame that also supported the steeple cab structure. In appearance the little juice jacks were like dozens of other little 70 tonners built before and after the turn of the century, but these were the first small locomotives ever built to run on 3,000 volts DC.

In the interests of standardization, many of the small components of these locomotives, such as pantagraphs, switches, headlights, heaters and air compressor, were interchangeable with the same components on the Class EF1 motors.

Rated at 510 horsepower, with a 14,000 lb. tractive effort, they could, for short periods, exert as much as 41,000 lbs. of tractive effort. The lowest geared electric locomotives on the railroad, with a ratio of 17:64, they normally work at speeds of around 10 mph, but if pushed hard are capable of a maximum of 35 mph.

Class EP2, Bi-polar

In 1919, with work well underway on the Othello-Tacoma electrification across the Cascades, the Milwaukee ordered fifteen passenger "motors" from Alco-GE and Baldwin-Westinghouse for the Coast Division and to replace the twelve modified freight motors then in passenger service on the Rocky Mountain sections of the line. These modified freight motors, Class EP1, which had been geared for a 60 mph top speed, fitted with train heating boilers and lighting equipment in 1915, were to be regeared and assigned to freight service on the Coast Division. The five new Alco-GE motors were to be used on the newly electrified Coast Division, and the ten Baldwin-Westinghouse motors would be assigned to passenger service between Avery and Harlowton on the Rocky Mountain and Missoula Divisions. While both of the new classes of passenger

A CLASS S2 Northern rolls ponderously out into 28th Street in Minneapolis, in August, 1949, and a Ford and a Pontiac wait respectfully for it to pass. The cast steel pilot and retracting coupler was designed specifically to ward off an automobile that might otherwise be caught on it and cause a derailment.

Jack Malven

THE EASTBOUND OLYMPIAN HIAWATHA awaits the highball at Spokane's Union Station. Train No. 16 is heavy this June evening in 1951, and the S-3 Northern has a helper, F-5 Pacific Number 889, coupled to its pilot to get the streamliner up the short heavy grade out of the Spokane River Valley to Manito.

Dr. Philip R. Hastings

power (Class EP2 Alco-GE and Class EP3 Baldwin-Westinghouse) were assigned to the same type of passenger service, the mechanical design and appearance of the locomotives was strikingly different.

Except perhaps for the famous streamlined Atlantics and Hudsons, used on the east end of the system in Hiawatha service, the locomotive to become most closely identified with the Milwaukee Road, in later years, was the Alco-GE Bi-polar. The Bi-polars were unique in design because the bi-polar fields for each motor were carried on the truck frame, allowing full freedom for vertical play of the armature between them, eliminating all gearing, armature and suspension bearings, jack shafts, side rods and other power transmitting devices. The inspiration for this design originated with the "gearless" electric locomotives used on the New York Central Railroad in its New York terminal, probably the first bi-polar type of electric locomotive where the axles served as the motor armatures, and the driving wheels were an integral part of the motor mechanism.

The five huge 265 ton, 3,240 hp. Bi-polars, designed specifically for passenger service in the Cascades, were highly efficient in high speed operation (about 10% more efficient than geared electric types at 50 mph) due to the motor armatures being built solidly on the driving axles, resulting in a low center of gravity, and were an immediate success when put into service between Othello and Tacoma in 1920.

Before actually entering service in 1920, the Bi-polars were extensively tested at the builder's plant in Erie, Pennsylvania. One such test, an exhibition of tractive effort and regenerative braking power of the big motors, would be termed a press demonstration today, but was nevertheless of very real interest to motive power men across the country. Locomotive 10251, first off the production line, was coupled nose to nose (to avoid pulled drawbars) to two modern steam locomotives. With throttles opened, the steam engines began to push the Bi-polar backwards down the tangent track. Then the controller of the Bi-polar was slowly advanced and began to draw current. Simultaneously, the throttles of the steam engines were opened wider, to the last notch, and as the controller of the electric was advanced still further, the steam engines began to huff and puff under an extraordinary strain, came to a complete stop, and then still straining as the controller of the Bi-polar was fully advanced, began to slide backwards.

In the regenerative braking demonstration the steam engines pushed the Bi-polar down the track until the regenerative braking was turned on. The steam engines slowed down as the braking was turned up to full power, and they fought to overcome the resistance of the regenerative braking. Finally, with their throttles wide open, they could barely move the Bi-polar, which in addition to demonstrat-

THE ALCO BUILT 2-6-0 Class M-2 No. 2976, in the Tacoma yards in 1927, was one of the relatively few Moguls owned by the Milwaukee Road, and was acquired from the Chicago Junction Railroad (No. 102). Later applied to much of the steam power of the railroad, the odd square shaped frame around the headlight lens became a distinguishing feature of Milwaukee steam engines.

Collection of Harold K. Vollrath

ing its remarkable braking power, had been returning power to the powerhouse during the entire demonstration.

A similar demonstration was conducted in Tacoma, before the press and Coast Division officials with locomotive 10254, against one of the 2-6-6-2 compounds in service on the Coast Division, and another was held on one of the high curved bridges in Snoqualmie Pass with the Bi-polars clearly victorious, and reams of copy poured forth from members of the press who had witnessed the events.

The Bi-polars were originally rated as capable of pulling a 960 ton load — twelve heavy weight steel passenger cars — up a 2% grade at 25 mph. In service testing resulted in an increased rating to 1,120 tons — fourteen cars — up a 2% grade at 25 to 27 mph — no mean feat for a single unit locomotive in 1920. Top speed was listed at 70 mph, but lightly loaded, they were fully capable of 80 mph.

The appearance of the Bi-polars was as unique as their mechanical design. Some of the officials on the Rocky Mountain Divisions, conditioned to the more conventional appearance of the boxcab type Baldwin-Westinghouse motors, felt that the Bi-polars with small 44" drivers simply didn't look like a passenger engine should, and referred to the Bi-polars as "caterpillars running on tracks." The low wheeled bi-polars, nevertheless, were slightly faster than the 68" drivered Baldwin-Westinghouse motors. Seventy-six feet long, with a three section articulated steeple cab mounted between long horseshoe shaped

hoods, they rolled on fourteen axles — twelve driving, two guiding — in a 1-B-D/D-B-1 wheel arrangement with enough articulation between the driving frames (the longest rigid wheelbase section was only 16'11") to allow them to follow heavy and reverse curvature like a snake gliding around obstacles in its path. The twelve powered axles were necessary, as were the low drivers, to insure sufficient pulling power. Both of these very different locomotives were powered by twelve motors, but while the Bi-polar rode on twelve single motor powered axles, the Baldwin-Westinghouse rode on six twin motor powered axles. Since the motors were an integral part of the axles on the Bi-polar, there was no way to power each axle with two motors through gearing as was done on the Baldwin-Westinghouse.

Running gear of the Bi-polars consisted of four individual trucks — two end trucks having three axles each and two center trucks having four axles each. The locomotives could be separated during shopping by removing the center cab and pulling the pin between the two eight wheel drive trucks, although the now separated units could not be operated independently. The four trucks were all connected by articulated joints that carried the magnetic circuit as well as the tractive and mechanical stresses. Their riding qualities were superb, due mainly to the design of the leading and trailing trucks, and the method of suspending the weight of the main or center cab which carried the oil fired train heating steam boiler, oil and water tanks, circulating pumps and a motor driven blower for forced draft. The successive trucks were coupled in such a way as to break up or dampen periodic oscillations or nosing caused by rough track, while the weight of the center cab was so suspended on the front and rear trucks (that carried one guiding axle and two driving axles) that any kick of the leading or trailing wheels against the track was cushioned by the movement of the center cab. Pounding of the track by Bi-polars was unheard of, and the 530,000 lb. locomotives rode as easily on the thinly ballasted 90 lb. rail of the Pacific Coast Railroad — through Maple Valley — into Seattle as they did on the heavier rail elsewhere.

The motors are relatively simple on an electric locomotive — the controls, auxiliaries and accessories are complex, and the 28' long hoods on each end housed a variety of equipment, including the 3,000 volt contactors, air compressor, resistor grids, circuit breakers, motor generator set, and an 80 volt storage battery for auxiliary power similar to that carried under passenger cars. Cover plates located along the rounded hoods provided access to equipment and were so located as to minimize accidental contact with high voltage. Only low voltage control circuits entered the operating cabs, and enginemen could pass from one cab to the other through the center cab without having to enter the high voltage compartments. Access to the resistor grids, relays and high voltage switching equipment was through a small door at the outer end of each hood with the equipment inside located on each side of a central passageway.

Control of the Bi-polars was very similar to the freight motors, except that the large motor-generator set, for providing traction motor field current during regeneration, was eliminated, and four of the traction motors were utilized as generators to furnish field current to the other eight traction motors during regeneration. The operating cabs at each end of the main cab contained the three section interlocking main controllers for power and regenerating control instruments, all braking controls and a small compressor operating off the battery circuit to raise the pantagraph when putting the locomotive into service. Over each operating cab was mounted a slider pantagraph of standard design with sand boxes directly beneath them. Like all other motors in service on the road, the frame was designed to take all pushing and pulling loads while the cabs and hoods "floated on the frame."

Outweighed by the slightly bigger Baldwins (310 to 265 tons) the Bi-polars, nevertheless, in starting tractive effort, outpulled the Baldwins by nearly 10,000 lbs. due to the fact that the Bi-polar put 458,000 lbs. on the drivers while the Baldwin-Westinghouse motors put 420,000 lbs. on the drivers. The Bi-polar was slightly faster also in both the continuous and hourly ratings, moving upgrade at 25 and 28.2 mph compared to 23.8 and 26 mph for the Baldwin. Tractive effort rating of the Bi-polars, like any electric locomotive hinged upon a number of variables, and upon whether you are talking about the continuous rating, one hour rating or maximum tractive effort. These variables, particularly in regard to the maximum tractive effort, included the condition of the track, the percentage of grade being pulled and whether the trolley voltage was up to the full 3,000 volts DC. Under ideal conditions, that is dry smooth rail, full trolley voltage, the Bi-polars were rated at exerting between 114,500 and 123,500 lbs. of maximum tractive effort at 25 and 30% coefficient of adhesion. This is about equal to a Norfolk and Western Class A 2-6-6-4. However, this maximum effort could be exerted for only a few minutes before the traction motors would fuse in a cloud of blue smoke due to tremendous overheating. The Bi-polars put 87.5% of their total weight (457,800 lbs.) on the drivers, but by spreading this weight out over twelve driving axles, only 38,150 lbs. pressed down on the rail compared to 70,000 lbs. per driving axle on the Baldwins. The Bi-polars total weight on the drivers exceeded the weight that the Baldwins put on the six driving axles by 37,800 lbs., yet the Baldwins total weight exceeded that of the Bi-polar design by nearly fifty tons. The continuous tractive effort was listed at 42,000 lbs. and the one hour rating at 48,000 lbs. on a 2% grade trailing a 960 ton train with a coefficient of adhesion on the ruling grade of 12.3%. Horsepower developed at the continuous and one hour ratings was 3,180 and 4,200.

CLASS H8 American type No. 41, was regularly assigned to the Hutchinson branch in Minnesota. While bucking heavy drifts of compacted snow on the run to Glencoe, in January, 1941, the Rogers built 4-4-0 lost its snowplow pilot, and was sent to the Minneapolis shops for repairs. Snow on top of the headlight, and completely plugging the large open area between the pilot beam and smokebox, is evidence of the heavy going that sheared off the plow.
Collection of Roger Lins

SHOP ENGINE X979 at Milwaukee in October, 1953.

Wally Swanson

Almost noiseless in operation, due to the lack of any gear noise, they emitted a low humming sound that became louder while moving upgrade and drawing large amounts of current. While on the level, they could ghost into a terminal or station such as Ellensburg virtually unnoticed except for the rumbling sound of the wheels on the rail, and the vibration of the earth. The high pitched, penetrating shrill of the air whistles on the Bi-polars, however, was a distinctive sound that could carry for miles on still air sounding for all the world like a peanut stand whistle. There was no mistaking the whistle of the Bi-polar, and it quickly became a trademark of the Milwaukee Road, the Olympian and the Columbian between Othello and Tacoma, and later, Seattle. In 1956, when the Bi-polars were transferred to work in Idaho and Montana on the Olympian Hiawatha, they were fitted with the familiar diesel air horns, and after nearly four decades the peanut whistles across the Cascades were gone.

Before the Bi-polars were transferred to Montana, attempts were made to utilize them in freight service since they were surplus motive power on the Coast Division when the Olympian Hiawatha was running straight through from the east with diesel power. Primarily these attempts failed because, first, the Bi-polar's frame would not stand the stresses of more than two of them coupled together, and secondly, because their lack of low speed gearing obviated their running for hour after hour in the 15 to 18 mph range while working with other freight motors. Attempting to run them at low speed, while drawing heavy amperage, could result only in serious overheating of the motors and ultimate failure.

Track clearance under the 30" diameter motors was close, but adequate. High water, of course, was not to the liking of the Bi-polars or to the liking of any other truck or axle mounted electric motor. Unlike steam power, they were not capable of wading through water over a few inches high. Permanent snow plows were mounted on both pilots, and while wet snow has always been a problem in the Cascades, it did not affect the low mounted motors.

The basically simple and uncomplicated Bi-polar design was exceptionally rugged and trouble free. When maintenance was necessary, the Bi-polar design and construction facilitated removal of the wheels and motor armature. Where on other designs it was necessary to pull the cab structure to get at the motor, on a Bi-polar it was a fairly simple job for shopmen to remove a pair of wheels for driver, tire or armature replacement. Spare drivers with armature in place were kept in reserve at Tacoma and Othello and one or more pair of drivers could be replaced during inspection with the locomotive returned to service in a couple of hours. The Bi-polars performed better than the original specifications called for, and they outlasted the Baldwins by several years. In a large part their longevity was due to their low maintenance cost. Before they were scrapped in the 1960's, after several years storage in Montana, it was estimated that it would have cost less than $2,000 per locomotive to put them back into heavy service.

Class EP3, Baldwin-Westinghouse

The order for the ten Baldwin-Westinghouse motors in 1919 for assignment to the Rocky Mountain and Missoula Divisions, was the only time the railroad stepped away from its favorite manufacturer, Alco-GE. The orders were divided between the Westinghouse and General Electric companies to hasten delivery dates because of the high cost of fuel oil. Both the Bi-polars and the Baldwins were designed for the same type of heavy passenger service, and the differences between them represented different approaches to the solution of an operating problem. The mechanical design of the Baldwin-Westinghouse motors, and their familiar boxcab layout, with a few curves around the cab and roof line, was nearly identical to the high speed electric passenger motors built in 1919 for the New York, New Haven & Hartford Railroad.

Neither unpleasing nor particularly distinctive in appearance, they could best be described as conventional and businesslike. They were by far the biggest single unit electric locomotives ever put into service on the Milwaukee Road. The monstrous Baldwins were 88' 7" long over the coupler faces, with a total wheel base of 79' 10", and the longest rigid wheel base 16' 9".

The 620,000 lb. units were nearly 100,000 lbs. heavier than the Bi-polars, but with 200,000 lbs. supported by six guiding axles in a 2-C1/1-C-2 (a long articulated joint couples the two driving frames) wheel arrangement, the Baldwins put less total weight on the driving axles than the Bi-polars. This resulted in a starting or maximum tractive effort of 105,000 lbs. at 25% coefficient of adhesion — considerably less than the Bi-polar's 123,500 lbs. However, the 3,400 continuous horsepower developed by the Baldwins at 26 mph was slightly greater than the 3,200 horsepower developed by the Bi-polars at 28.4 mph, and the one hour rating was 4,200 horsepower. From an operating standpoint the difference was small and of little importance.

The Baldwin-Westinghouse motors were a "quill spring drive" design, and their running gear with 4-6-2 wheel arrangement and 68" drivers (unusually large for a gear driven locomotive) has been described as two Pacifics joined back to back. A hollow tube or quill surrounded the axle and passed through bearings mounted on the frame of the motor, the clearance between the axle and the hollow tube being sufficient to permit considerable movement of the axle relative to the quill. Concentrically arranged coil springs were attached between the projecting arms on the quill and the spokes of the drive wheel. The basic function of the drive wheel mounted coil springs was to absorb starting and slipping shocks to prevent them from being transmitted directly to the twin motors, and to minimize gear wear. The drive was flexible in both directions of rotation as well as vertically.

EXCEPT FOR TWO Class D-1 0-8-0's and the electric steeple cab switchers, switching types on the Milwaukee were of the 0-6-0 wheel arrangement, Classes I-5 and I-6, and numbered in the 1400 and 1500 series. They were built as hand fired coal burners, but those in service in the far West were converted to burn oil. Reliable and simple little engines, their one claim to distinction was probably the unusual running board and hand rail arrangement on the fireman's side, as shown on No. 1507.
Collection of Wally Swanson

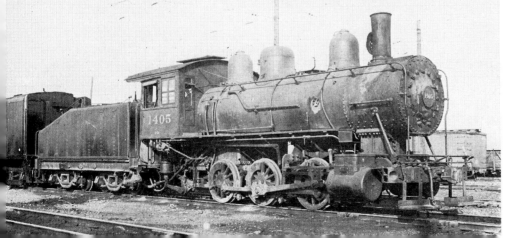

REFUTING THE WIDESPREAD NOTION that old hard working steam locomotives, in every day service, resembled rolling scrap heaps held together by dirt, stains and rust patches, are two photographs, taken in the 1950's in the Tacoma yards by W. Wilkinson. No. 1490, a forty year old veteran switcher, gleams in late afternoon sunlight, and No. 64, a modernized Mallet, used in "chain gang service," shows little evidence of hard use or lack of care.

The twin 750 volt motors, mounted in pairs above the driving axle on the locomotive frame, were fitted with small pinion gears that drove a large gear attached to the quill. With 24 teeth on the pinions and 89 on the quill gear (expressed as 24:89 ratio) the armature will rotate 3.29 times for each time the driver rotates. The more revolutions the pinion gear had to turn to make the driving wheel revolve once, the more powerful the locomotive would be. Conversely, the fewer revolutions the pinion gear had to revolve to turn the drive wheel once, the less powerful, but faster the locomotive would be. It was desirable to rotate the motor at a high enough speed to obtain maximum motor efficiency, but limited to below the point where too high a rotational speed and the resulting centrifugal force would damage the motor itself. The driving components were of good design and manufacture, and the locomotives gave little trouble during almost forty years of service. From the very start, however, the locomotive frames were troublesome and had to be returned to the manufacturer for rebuilding just after they entered service.

The cabs of the Baldwin-Westinghouse motors "floated" on the running gear, and all tractive effort loads were transmitted through the running gear frames. All cabs, except No. 10300 which was rebuilt, were of rigid design and did not articulate as the Bi-polars did. The engineer and fireman operating compartments were built at each end of the cab, and all the auxiliary equipment, train heating boiler, and fuel and water tanks were located between.

The electro-pneumatic control equipment was actuated from the master controller by control current at 85 volts supplied by a motor generator set. The motor generator, in conjunction with two axle generator sets and a storage battery, furnished current for such auxiliaries as the air compressor and train lighting. Axle generators, one located on each leading truck, furnished current for exciting the traction motor fields during regeneration.

Each Bi-polar and Baldwin-Westinghouse cost the Milwaukee Road around $200,000 for a total of $3,000,000, a heavy expenditure for power by any railroad in the 1920's. For the same sum, two to three times as many steam locomotives could have been purchased, but after eight years of operation, railroad figures showed far less cost for fuel and crews, and maintenance costs reduced by about one third compared to the maintenance costs of steam power.

The Baldwin-Westinghouse motors were scrapped shortly after the Korean War, several years before the Bi-polars were scrapped. Heavy maintenance costs were incurred on the Baldwins because of their lack of a "flash" boiler for train heating purposes.

"HALF-UNIT" FREIGHT LOCOMOTIVE at Rockdale, Washington just west of Snoqualmie Pass tunnel, 1920.
The Milwaukee Road

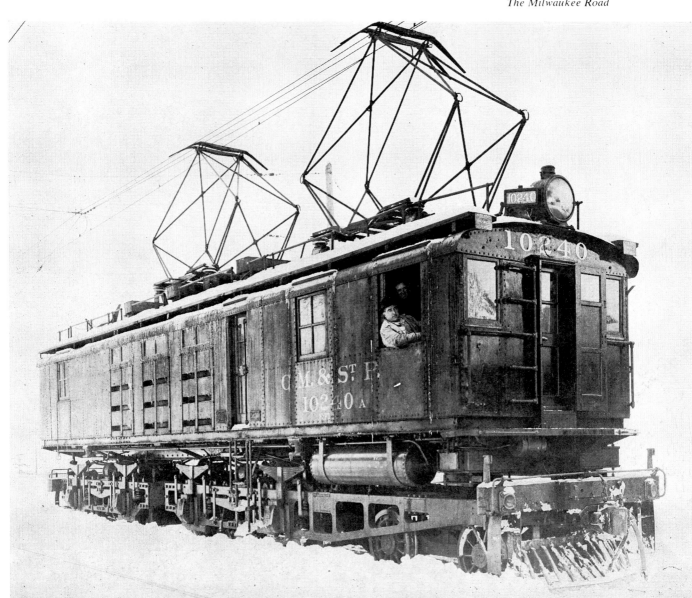

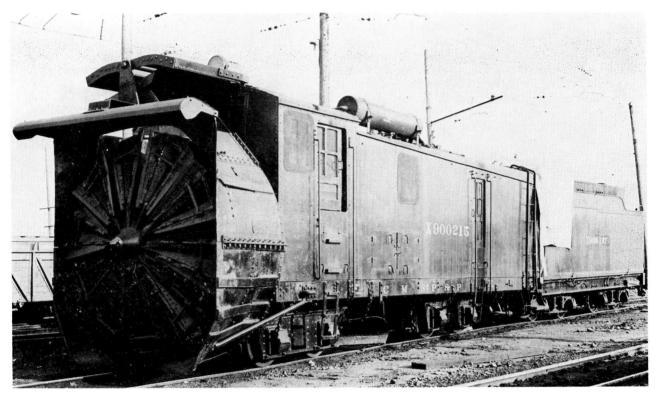

STEAM POWERED, OIL FIRED rotary snow plow X900215, with accompanying tender, waits in the yards at Tacoma in 1953. The heavy steel mesh bolted across the windows was designed to prevent a wall of sliding snow and debris from punching out the windows and suffocating the crew inside.

Collection of Wally Swanson

The antiquated boiler arrangement on the Baldwin motors caused the locomotive cabs to continually fill with oil soot, that in turn caused trouble with the electrical auxiliaries. The Baldwins also suffered from weak frames that precluded their being used as multiple units, although they were often double-headed with a crew in each cab.

Class EF4, Little Joe

The finest electric locomotives on the Milwaukee Railroad today, are the twelve Class EF4 locomotives, originally built by Alco-GE after World War II for the Russian government for use on its 5' gauge railroads. The EF4's were never delivered. With the advent of the Cold War, the United States clamped an embargo on certain types of essential equipment and material going to Russia. Alco-GE had wide experience in designing basic locomotives for multiple gauge use, and the EF4's, although built for a 5' gauge, were adaptable to our 4' 8½" gauge. So twelve of the "Little Joes," as they were nicknamed, were bought by the Milwaukee, and others by the South Shore, and converted to 4' 8½" gauge for use on our track. The remainder were sold to Brazil for use on their 63" gauge Paulista Railroad. In addition to changing the gauge of the running gear, two of the locomotives, E-20 and E-21, were fitted with train heating boilers for passenger use, and all were painted in Milwaukee colors of orange and maroon.

With the scrapping of the Baldwins after the Korean War, the "Little Joes," 87 feet 9 inches long and weighing 586,600 pounds, became the biggest, the heaviest and the most powerful single unit locomotives on the railroad. At 25 mph the big units are rated at 77,000 lbs. tractive effort on a continuous rating, and will exert 110,750 lbs. starting, at 25% adhesion. Two EF4's, with a GP9 cut in, operating as multiple units, will develop some 12,500 horsepower. A single unit is rated at over 5,500 horsepower, and it is possible to concentrate as many as four of them on the head end operating multiple unit for a total of 22,000 hp.

With an elongated "Bulldog" type nose, the EF4's resembled some of the early diesel units, but the car body, the large pantagraphs, and 2-D/D-2 running gear made them close cousins to the GE built Class W electrics used on the Great Northern. The car body floated or was suspended on top of the running gear with the tractive effort and stresses transmitted entirely through the running gear.

The EF4's are the only truly dual service electric locomotives on the Milwaukee Road. Powered by eight 1,500 volt motors geared to a 21:80 ratio, and turning 47" drivers, they can attain a top speed of 84 mph. Two of the units equipped with steam heat boilers (since removed) operated on the head end of both the Columbian and the Olympian Hiawatha.

In freight service, the EF4's have been so satisfactory in operation that they have virtually taken over all electric powered main line freight service between Harlowton and Avery. Usually running as two units, they are also coupled with a GP9 for additional power to pull over the humps without requiring a separate helper locomotive.

A miniaturized diesel control system was added to the controls of the EF4 locomotives mounted to the right of the electric panel. Designed by Mr. Wylie, Milwaukee Road electrical engineer, the sys-

THE ENGINEER OF A WESTBOUND extra at Othello, Washington looks back along his train from the cab of E-36, a four unit freight motor, Class EF4 and waits for the highball.

Casey Adams

tem has been simple and effective in operation. When the additional tractive effort of the diesel is required on grades, the diesel engine is cut in to assist the two electrics. When the locomotives are over the top of the grade, the diesel is shut down and the electrics proceed in regenerative braking down the hill. Further modification was required to allow the diesel to use its dynamic braking while the electrics were in regenerative braking.

Purchased at bargain prices, and immediately adaptable to an existing electrical plant, the "Little Joes" probably helped to prevent scrapping of the electrification in the 1950's. That plant, although still in useable condition, was outdated and operating with locomotives nearly forty years old. The old electrics were still serviceable, but their usual 15 mph uphill and 30 mph downhill was a handicap to the railroad that needed to get out and run to compete with its diesel powered and fast running neighbors, the Great Northern and Northern Pacific. With millions of miles of service now, the fast running EF4's have demonstrated their ability to compete with the dieselized systems.

Class EP1, E-22 and E-23

In 1950, when the twelve dual service "Little Joes" went into service on the Rocky Mountain Division, they created a surplus of both freight and passenger locomotives. At first, it was thought that a number of the elderly freight units would be scrapped, but after considering the operating and maintenance advantages of these old geared units, it was decided that four of them (later five) would be converted into two, two unit passenger locomotives. The units selected, and set aside at Tacoma for conversion, were originally equipped with water tanks, when they worked passenger trains in the Rockies.

Tacoma was selected to do the conversion work because the shop force had a vast amount of experience in rebuilding electric locomotives that had been damaged in slides and other accidents. One of the locomotives selected for conversion had been through the Tacoma shops twice before. No. 10208 first rolled into the Tacoma shops in 1920, as dismantled parts loaded into gondolas after being rolled 600 feet down the side of a mountain into heavy timber, after striking a slide between Hyak and Cedar Falls, Washington. In 1936, 10208 (now renumbered 10505), was involved in another snowslide between Hyak and Cedar Falls at Bandera, Washington (now the site of an emergency airfield) and again rolled into the heavy timber. It was picked up once more and sent to Tacoma for rebuilding.

Locomotive 10103 was also a veteran of Coast Division freight service, both as a helper on Beverly Hill, and as a road locomotive. Like 10208, 10103 had been in passenger service on the Rocky Mountain Division before being converted to a freighter. These two veterans had rolled up nearly 700,000 miles as passenger locomotives, and an additional nearly two and three quarter million miles on the Coast Division in freight service.

In the 1939 renumbering program 10103 became E-69, and 10208 became E-28. As converted freight locomotives the E-69 became the three unit E-23A-B-C and the E-28 became E-22A-B, both Class EP1-A.

Although all five units received nearly identical equipment during the conversion, the first to be converted, the E-22, was the most radically changed in outward appearance. E-22 received a semi-streamlined cab and modernized body shell that gave it a decided foreign look. Electrical equipment was modified, as well as the gearing, and the locomotive was capable of 70 mph with power equal to that of a 4,500 hp diesel. One of the most interesting changes

THE REAR VIEW of a single unit freight motor shows the switching type pilot and the steps added for local freight service.

The Milwaukee Road

A MILWAUKEE ROAD SHOP supervisor examines the front truck of an EF-5 box-cab freight locomotive at the Tacoma engine house prior to its beginning an eastbound trip. The seemingly indestructible motors, built around 1915, still power an extra movement every day. Due to the limited swing of the front truck inside the frame, the big units are restricted to nothing tighter than a 21 degree curve.

Robert E. Oestreich

made was the replacement of the original four wheel lead trucks with roller bearing engine trucks taken from scrapped F7 Hudsons.

Locomotive E-23, although not outwardly as modern looking as the E-22, received the same mechanical changes. The pilot assembly and the front of the cabs were changed slightly. Union Pacific colors of yellow and gray with the old style headlight mounted on top of the cab (but with new multiple sealed beams fitted in a square pattern) made the locomotive appear much as it had when first built.

Redesigned to power the Olympian Hiawatha during those periods when the diesels were not run through from Chicago to the coast, the rebuilt electrics, in large measure due to their extremely low maintenance costs, could be operated as cheaply as twenty cents a mile, in heavy passenger service in the mountains.

Diesels

In the fall of 1941, the Milwaukee Road began the replacement of its steam power with the delivery of a pair of EMD E6 passenger units that were put into service on the Hiawathas and train No. 57, mail and express, between Chicago and Minneapolis. A pair of Alco-GE passenger units — No. 14 — closely followed E6 No. 15 into similar service. Both locomotives, rated at 4,000 horsepower, demonstrated throughout World War II an ability to make time and to keep a tight schedule. Even more interesting to the railroad, they displayed a fantastic ability to operate under quick turnaround conditions (as little as 90 minutes) day in and day out, with only routine servicing, demonstrating the same advantages over steam that the electrics had demonstrated nearly

three decades before. The diesels had the additional advantage, however, of carrying their own generating plant right on board the locomotive, eliminating the need for a costly investment in fixed plant-sub-stations, catenary and all the other appurtances required by straight electrics. The diesels, although far more costly than modern steam power, quickly paid for themselves in reduced maintenance and fuel costs, vastly increased availability, and an ability to start and pull a heavy train at almost any speed desired.

Actually the Milwaukee had been dabbling in diesel, or more correctly "gas-electric," power for some time prior to the delivery of Nos. 14 and 15 to main line service. Several classes of light motor cars had been in service on the lightly trafficked branches since the 1920's and early 1930's. All were somewhat erratic in performance, however, displaying a propensity to break down, and while they saved the cost of a steam engine and coaches, their dependability left much to be desired. Therefore the splendid performance of Nos. 14 and 15 in main line service, was a real eye opener to the Milwaukee.

The Milwaukee had observed the advantages of diesel power in fast passenger service on the line of its competitor and neighbor the Chicago Burlington and Quincy. The Zephyr service between Chicago and the Twin Cities had been giving the road all the competition it could ask for, and the early shovel nosed Zephyr power units had displayed a remarkable availability and fast running characteristics. In fact, the Milwaukee had seriously considered turning to diesel power in 1938, instead of staying with steam power and ordering the F7 Hudsons.

In 1940, the door opened a bit when some GE built forty-four ton locomotives, very limited in their capabilities, were ordered for light industrial switching service, and in 1941, when the road re-

EXTRA E60 WEST — 125 CARS following the boxcab freight motors — emerges from the tunnel near Ravenna, Montana along the Clark Fork River on February 23, 1942. The tranquil mountain stillness is broken only by the deep hum of the motors, and by the tramp of the cars as they thump and clatter over the frog of the siding switch. The automatic block signal has winked from clear green to cautious amber to warning red as electronic relays respond to E60's approach from the east.

W. R. McGee

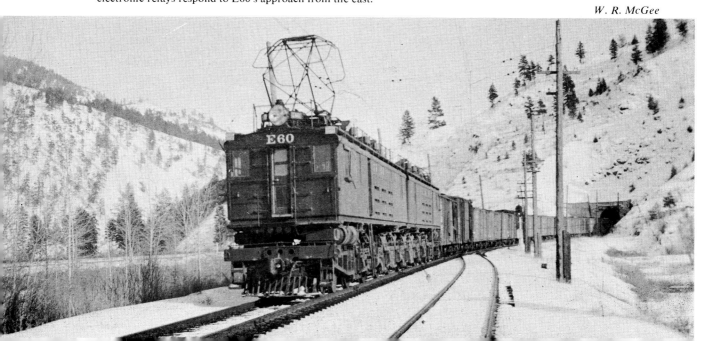

A FREIGHT MOTOR SHUFFLES CARS at Black River junction on a summer evening in 1956 as the engineer looks down at the photographer. The forty year old locomotive looks little worse for wear, and in 1970, some of the units are still in daily service.

Robert E. Oestreich

ceived its first EMD FT type freighter from the Electro-Motive plant in LaGrange, Ill. The big freighter was composed of two semi-permanently coupled A and B units that weighed in at 923,000 lbs., with all the weight on the drivers. The 5,400 horsepower locomotive could exert a starting tractive effort of 230,800 lbs. at 25% adhesion, and had a top speed of seventy miles per hour. It immediately started rolling up ton-miles at a rate that completely outclassed every steam engine on the road. Even doubleheaded modern steam power could not keep up with the power and availability, nor compete with the cheaper operating and maintenance costs of this four unit internal combustion locomotive that looked

like four short passenger cars coupled together. Crew costs were halved, and the FT freighter could run clear through to the coast with only refueling necessary. At speed it was as easy on the track as the big Bi-polars, something that couldn't be said for the steamers, that when pushed hard, could kink and pound track unmercifully. Twelve more of the FT freighters were delivered between 1942 and 1945, and if the road had had its choice in 1944, when the Class S3 Northerns were delivered, it would have chosen more FT diesels. Also except that passenger diesel units were not being built for the duration of the war, E6's and Alcos would have replaced all the Atlantics and Hudsons in main line service.

One thousand horsepower switchers, built by Baldwin, started arriving in 1942, with the same story of needing only routine servicing and little maintenance, a far cry from the continuous servicing and maintenance required by the old Mikes, Consolidations and 0-6-0's used in switching and transfer service. Fairbanks Morse switchers, also one thousand horsepower units, were delivered in 1945, and in 1946 and 1947, Fairbanks Morse delivered seven, two thousand horsepower, passenger units to power the new Olympian Hiawatha and other runs. They were odd looking locomotives, chrome trim and color scheme notwithstanding, and they had severe enough problems with their diesel engines to result in their downgrading to secondary runs, after only a few short months of service. The continuing engine problems led to scrapping of all the units a few years later.

The initial demonstration of diesel power running clear through to the Pacific Coast on a regularly scheduled basis, was impressive enough to jeopardize the continuimg existence of the electrification in the far West, but the purchase of the twelve Little Joes in 1950, demonstrated to the road, the even greater capacity of modern dual service electric power.

The Little Joes, still running, forestalled any decision to scrap the electric plant, and the only problem that they created was that there were not enough of them. They were purchased at a very good price, and twinges of regret have been felt in the electrification department that the road did not purchase the entire lot.

In the late 1940's and during the 1950's, diesels arrived from all of the major builders in ever increasing numbers, but the lion's share came from EMD, who supplied the road with a variety of hood and "covered wagon" styles. Six wheel truck SD7 and SD9 units, that could step lightly on the seventy pound rail and wooden trestles, were ordered to replace the old steamers like the Mallet compounds, on the branch lines. The last of the steamers were replaced by the mid 1950's, and there was no place for them to go except temporary storage and then scrap lines to be cut up.

In 1972, the lion's share of the locomotive roster is still represented by EMD, but a large fleet of GE U-boats are in service, as well as Alco built units. Passenger service, except for the commuter trains out of Chicago and the Amtrak service between the Twin Cities and Chicago, is gone.

AT VENDOME, MONTANA, EAST of Butte, Milwaukee Extra E-36 East holds to 25 mph. under the regenerative brake of the EF-5 motor on a 2% descending grade into the Jefferson River Valley.

Philip C. Johnson

DIESEL/Electric rotary plows out the main and passing tracks on the west side of Snoqualmie Pass near Bandera.
Collection of Charles R. Wood

AT CEDAR FALLS, HELPER E-33 cuts in behind heavy tonnage about to ascend Snoqualmie Pass from the west. Markers, still in place on the last unit, indicate that the helper has come from the east side of the pass, after helping another train up the grade from Easton to Hyak. It is common practice to cut in the helper about one third of the way back in the train to equalize the strain on drawbars while working up the 2% gradient. Helper engineers became highly skilled at watching the drawbar action of the car immediately ahead of the locomotive to judge the effectiveness of their help to the road locomotive.

Stuart B. Hertz

ELECTRIC POWERED SHOP GOAT X3800, on the turntable at Deer Lodge in 1966, towing Little Joe E77, is surely the shortest shop goat in the history of railroading.

W. R. McGee

IN A LOGGED over area, high in the misty Cascade Mountains in Washington, a brand new Bi-polar pauses during an official test trip in 1920. Metal "extra" white flags are mounted below the classification lamps, and a cloud of white steam rises from the safety pops of the train heat boiler located in the center cab. Amazingly flexible for a large locomotive, the Bi-polars were exceptionally easy riding and easy too on the 90 lb. rail of this era.

Asahel Curtis

GE-253-A 1500/3000 VOLT commutating pole motor, used in both the EF-1 and EP-1 locomotives.

The Milwaukee Road

MILWAUKEE EXTRA E-49 West, light helper, crests the Continental Divide as it heads into the east portal of the summit tunnel, tunnel No. 11, Pipestone Pass.

Philip C. Johnson

GENERAL ELECTRIC BUILT BOXCAB passenger units pause at Deer Lodge, Montana in 1915 on the point of a transcontinental run just after opening of the electrification in Montana. The electrification, successful from the first day of operation, served as a model for other electrification programs throughout the world.

General Electric Company

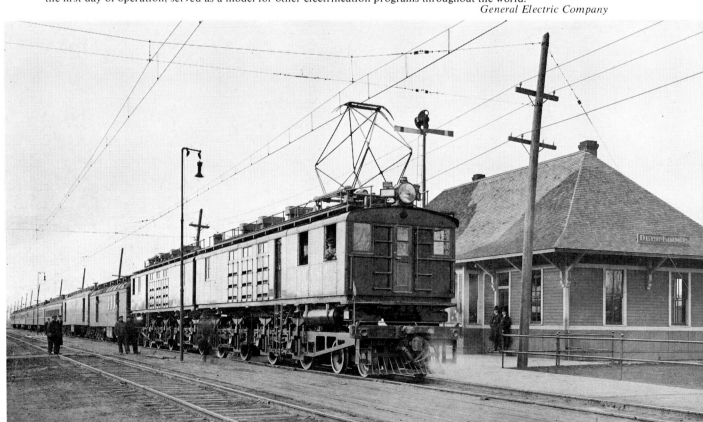

AT BUTTE, switcher E-82 works the Milwaukee-Butte Anaconda & Pacific interchange. The heavy steeple cab switchers are powerful, and with four 255 h.p. motors, E-82 can exert 42,000 lbs. of tractive effort for short periods.

Philip C. Johnson

(OPPOSITE) THE ENGINEER OF A BOX-CAB freight motor gently notches out the throttle, as an Othello bound extra freight starts to move out of the Tacoma yards. When the box-cabs were first put into service during World War I, the engineers had not yet learned not to yank the throttle wide open, the usual practice with steam engines on the head end of heavy tonnage, and their tremendous draw bar pull left the drawheads of fragile freight equipment scattered along the right of way between Three Forks and Donald.

Robert E. Oestreich

THE OLYMPIAN DRIFTS DOWNGRADE through Snoqualmie Pass on the west side of the Cascades in 1920. The main line through this area is actually single track supplemented by lengthy passing sidings that permit upgrade run around moves by faster trains, and provide a holding area for freight trains descending the pass to cool their wheels.

Asahel Curtis

RAILROAD PHOTOGRAPHS, PAINTINGS, CALENDERS, and timetables of the steam era generally followed a traditional format that featured a preponderance of posed head on views of locomotives, usually on a multiple track main line with the eagle eyed engineer leaning out of the cab, on the alert for the first sign of a minor malfunction. A refreshing change from the standard format is this photograph from the 1920's by the noted commercial photographer Asahel Curtis of a Bi-polar approaching Black River Junction. It is posed, and the engineer still leans out of the cab in the cold rain of a winter morning, but the camera angle moves to the side of the locomotive to bring us close to the mass and muscle of railroading with a dramatic display of the sheet steel, rivets, springs, journals and ponderous assemblies that comprise a modern "giant of the rails."

BI-POLARS WERE NICKNAMED "caterpillars and centipedes" by Milwaukee men on the more easterly electrified divisions of the Road, and Bi-polar E-3, with the Olympian in tow, shows why as she displays her fourteen low drivers and assorted hardware in the slanting rays of the sun.

Casey Adams

ENROUTE TO UNION STATION, a troop train of heavy Pullmans, in the distinctive orange and maroon easily identifiable as Milwaukee Road equipment, pulls through the yard in Georgetown (Seattle) in 1953. Bi-polar E-4 has yet to undergo the modernization program that will send it east to the Rocky Mountain Division to power the Olympian Hiawatha.

Collection of Wally Swanson

THE RAILROAD, JUSTIFIABLY PROUD of the big Bi-polars, made every effort to capitalize. on their publicity value. Enlarged many times, hand colored or tinted, and mounted in an elaborate frame, this widely reproduced publicity photograph of the new Bi-polar at the head of the Olympian on a curve in the Cascades, could be found in nearly every Milwaukee ticket office or business office throughout the country.

A COMPARISON BETWEEN THE OLYMPIAN of 1920 and the Olympian Hiawatha of the 1950's (below) shows the motive power, a Bi-polar, the same, but the streamlined, light weight equipment vastly different. The most interesting difference is in the photograph itself, with the Olympian Hiawatha coming upgrade in a cloud of dust rising from the roadbed, rather than the static picture of an entire train posed against a mountain backdrop. The entire impression is one of speed and a sense of urgency — quite a contrast to the 1920 photo.

Both Photos The Milwaukee Road

A FLARE HAS JUST STOPPED the eastbound Olympian Hiawatha at Cedar Falls at the beginning of its climb up Snoqualmie Pass, because of a snowslide that has plugged the main. It is raining hard here on this November day in 1955, and the dark sky is an indication of what may be expected at higher elevations.

Robert E. Oestreich

139

PHOTOGRAPHED near the Tacoma shops of the Milwaukee where the modernization work was done, Bi-polar E-5, painted in glossy black, light gray, orange and maroon, is ready for service on the head end of the Olympian Hiawatha.

The Milwaukee Road

MODERNIZED AND complete with diesel air horns, Bi-polar E-5 waits on the ready track at Deer Lodge for an assignment. The Bi-polars were sent to the Rocky Mountain Division for passenger service, and then were tried out briefly in freight service — for which they were never designed. They ended their nearly forty years of service sitting in dead storage beside the shops in Deer Lodge until they were scrapped in the early 1960's.

Collection of Don Dietrich

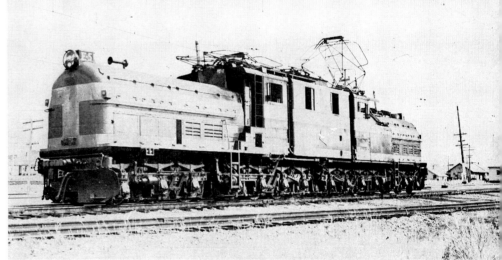

MORNING — AND the modernized Bi-polars hustle the westbound Olympian Hiawatha through the Kent Valley between Seattle and Tacoma. The unusual sight of the observation car running immediately behind the engines was necessitated by the stub-end terminal in Seattle, where the engines were switched to a parallel track, run around the train and coupled to the observation car to draw the train backwards to Tacoma. In the afternoon the procedure was reversed with the Hiawatha drawn backwards to Seattle where the engines were again switched to the head end of the train for the trip east.

Casey Adams

THE HEADEND CREWS chat as extras E-52 and E-71 West wait in Butte yard for the passage of the Olympian Hiawatha. The heavy steel to the far left contrasts with the lighter steel of the yard tracks, and illustrates the use of the term "high iron" when referring to the main line. After the passing of the "varnish," both freights, on a close headway, will resume their runs on the single track high iron.

Philip C. Johnson

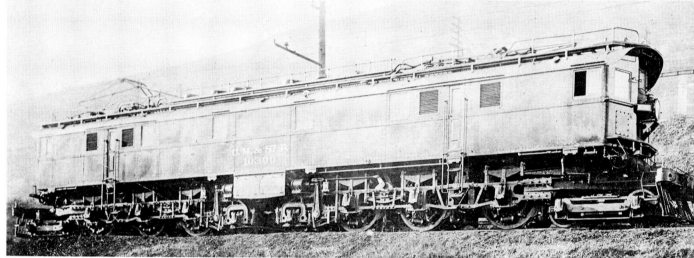

THE WEAK FRAME THAT CAUSED MUCH trouble just after the Baldwin-Westinghouse passenger motors entered service in 1920, is clearly evident in this early photo of the first unit to arrive for service on the Rocky Mountain Divisions.

Collection of Charles R. Wood

CLEARLY VISIBLE IN THIS photo is the greatly strengthened frame of Baldwin built passenger motor E15 on the head end of train No. 15, the Olympian, at Deer Lodge in 1940. It makes an interesting comparison with the photo of the same class locomotive as originally delivered to the road in 1920.

Don Dietrich

AT AVERY, IDAHO A PAIR of Baldwin-Westinghouse passenger motors lock couplers with a long and heavy eastbound troop train during World War II. Formidable looking locomotives, the big electrics were returned to the builder shortly after entering service in 1920 for strengthening of the frames. Although fast and powerful, they were scrapped shortly after the Korean War due to a doubleheading restriction, a recurrent problem with the train heat boilers, and because — like the Bi-polars — they lacked multiple unit connections so that one crew could operate two locomotives.

Casey Adams

BALDWIN-WESTINGHOUSE MOTOR E-14 awaits assignment to the eastbound Columbian at Avery. Motor E-14, formerly numbered 10305, carries a bronze plaque on the side of the locomotive just behind and below the engineer's cab that reads:

"Chicago, Milwaukee and St. Paul Ry.
To Puget Sound — Electrified
July 2, 1923
Warren G. Harding
President of the United States
Operated Locomotive No. 10305
Westbound Sappington, Mont.
to Avery, Idaho"

Philip C. Johnson

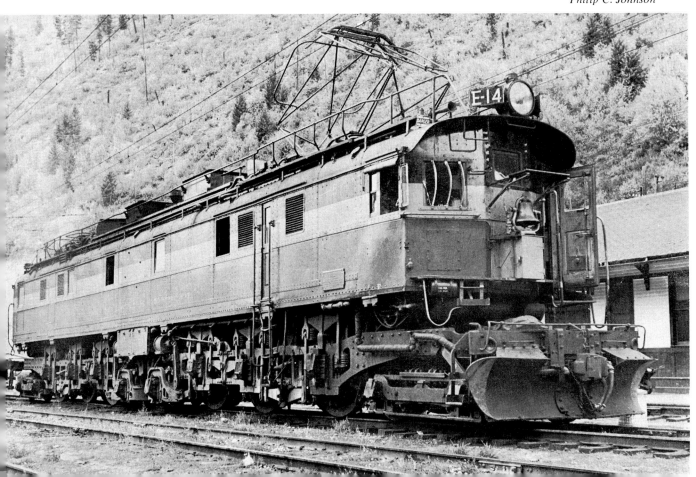

WITH AN AUXILIARY HEATER car coupled behind, Little Joe E-21, one of two assigned to passenger service, slides easily through a main line turnout at Harlowton, before picking up the westbound Olympian Hiawatha. The Little Joes, with their 80 mph speed capability, were splendid passenger power as well as extremely capable freight power.

L. C. Bellows

AT TWO DOT, Montana, the hogger of a Little Joe waits for a meet with a westbound freight out of Harlowton.
Martin Erickson
The Milwaukee Road

THROUGH A FROZEN LANDSCAPE painted in winter white, two Little Joes and a Geep move a time freight towards Butte yard in March of 1962. In the background, a huge smelter stack spews forth its smoke, an indication of the industrial activity in this, one of the richest copper mining and smelting areas in the world.

Jim Scribbins

A SINGLE LITTLE JOE, CLASS EF-4, leads Extra E-78 East through a short tunnel east of Alberton, Montana on the way to Missoula.

Philip C. Johnson

TRAIN 18, THE Columbian speeds along behind a "Little Joe," motor E-21, in August, 1953, east of St. Regis, Montana. This fine overhead shot of E-21 reveals not only the complex pantagraph assemblies on top of the big motor, but also the details of the lineside power poles and catenary.

Philip C. Johnson

EXTRA E-71 EAST ASSEMBLES its train in Butte yard for the stiff climb to Pipestone Pass, while a three unit helper and switcher, E-81 with the caboose, stay out of the way of the heavy road power.

Philip C. Johnson

AT BONNER JUNCTION, MONTANA, passenger extra E-21 East, a "Luther League Special" with fourteen coaches of teen-agers bound for a convention in Missoula, rolls beside the Clark Fork River. The special is powered by a combination rarely seen on the Rocky Mountain Division, an EP-4 class motor E-21 leading and an unidentified EF-4 class freight motor with a heater car (an ex-steam loco tender) coupled behind.

Philip C. Johnson

ON MAY 23, 1966, Little Joe E-78 suffered extensive damage from a spill onto rocks in Sixteen Mile Canyon. The smashed locomotive was taken to the Milwaukee shops where the shell of the locomotive was scrapped. New diesel cab assemblies were purchased from General Motors, and the rebuild shop forces custom fabricated the rest of the body.
The Milwaukee Road

THE REBUILD CAPABILITIES OF THE TACOMA SHOPS IS EVIDENCED IN THIS FEBRUARY 26, 1953 photograph of E22. The locomotive had rolled into the shops as a thirty-five year old freight motor, and emerged some weeks later a modernized and modified high speed passenger motor developing 5,000 horsepower, for service on the head end of the Olympian Hiawatha. In the fall of 1953, another old freight motor emerged as E23. Both locomotives, at one time, had served as passenger motors, but had been converted to freight after delivery of the Baldwins in 1920.

The Milwaukee Road

5,000 H.P. - 3,CCC V. D.C. high speed electric passenger locomo
No. E-22 and workmen at Tacoma Shops, C.M.St.P.&P. R.R. Company
February 26, 1953. This locomotive was converted from freight
which had been in service for 35 years.

UNDERGOING TESTS in the Cascades after an extensive rebuilding, E-22 pauses near the summit before taking an official train back downgrade to Tacoma, in February, 1953.
W. C. Janssen

THE "BIG HOOKS" have been called out to pick up the pieces after a derailment in Montana in the 1920's has reduced boxcars to kindling wood and scattered the boxcab motors about like children's toys. One motor is upside down in the foreground, and two others are jack-knifed across the tracks. Overhead catenary is looped like a lariat on the far main, while the overhead to the left is tangled into a fishing reel snarl. Damage is heavy, but after repair at the shops at Deer Lodge, the only evidence of the derailment will be the fresh paint on the motors when they are returned to service.
Ron Nixon

THE WESTBOUND OLYMPIAN CROSSES the Cedar River in September, 1956, trailing behind the very different looking semi-streamlined two unit E22. Modernized in the Tacoma shops in 1953, E23 received essentially the same treatment, but later picked up an old regeared "C" unit to make it a more powerful three unit locomotive. E22 was later repainted in yellow and red, removing the cross effect of the paint on the front and improving the rather continental look.

Robert E. Oestreich

RECONVERTED ONCE AGAIN TO a higher speed passenger motor, modernized, semi-streamlined freight motor E23, with the Olympian Hiawatha stretched out behind, waits for a green block along Houser Street in Renton, Washington in October, 1958, before proceeding east toward Maple Valley and Snoqualmie Pass.
Robert E. Oestreich

MODERNIZED AND SEMI-STREAMLINED E-22 awaits assignment at Avery — probably the eastbound Olympian Hiawatha. Replacing the old brass bearing lead truck, and just visible under the frame behind the pilot, is the roller bearing lead truck off of one of the Hudsons.

W. C. Janssen

GENERAL ELECTRIC BUILT GAS-ELECTRIC car Number 5903, shown at Cologne, Minnesota in June, 1940, is similar to Pullman built cars Numbers 5900 and 5901, modified for service on the electrified divisions as "troubleshooters." The huge headlight, mounted over the unusual V shaped front end designed to cut through deep snow, gave the car a Cyclops appearance. The profusion of smokejacks, exhaust stacks and radiators on the roof, represented attempts by the shops to correct a multitude of mechanical and cold weather problems.

Collection of Roger Lins

BUILT BY DAVENPORT (IOWA) Locomotive Works in 1942, switcher No. 1709, along with switcher No. 1708, was Caterpillar diesel engine powered. Switchers 1700 and 1701, built by G.E., and switchers 1702-1707, built by Whitcomb Locomotive Works, were very similar. Small and stubby, all of them were fitted with two engines that developed 180 to 190 hp. each. Rated at 22,000 lbs. of tractive effort and a maximum speed of 30 mph., they could work on curves as tight as 75 foot radius.

Collection of Don Dietrich

DAILY COEUR D'ALENE BRANCH freight, powered by a GE 44 ton diesel, switches "chip cars" at Coeur d'Alene on jointly used Great Northern track, in 1948. The elderly truss rod cars being switched, were owned by the old Spokane International, and were the home built product of the SI shops in Spokane.

Philip C. Johnson

PHOTOGRAPHED AT BENSENVILLE, Illinois in February, 1941, Engine No. 90 Class GE-1, an "0-8-0" switcher, built by Whitcomb in the 1930's, was certainly one of the weirdest locomotives on the Milwaukee roster.
Collection of Roger Lins

RAILCAR 5925, GAS-ELECTRIC, stands at the Milwaukee shops in Cedar Rapids, Iowa in 1948.

Don Dietrich

A NEW FOUR UNIT FT TYPE temporarily separated into two locomotives for test purposes faces the setting sun at Aberdeen, South Dakota. The handsome winged emblem on the front of the units unfortunately did not last long and as succeeding types were delivered the color scheme and decorations became more utilitarian.

Casey Adams

ON JULY 13, 1947, THE NEW streamlined Olympian Hiawatha, with Fairbanks Morse diesel power on the head end, meets the old Olympian, now the Columbian, under the catenary at Three Forks, Montana. Streamlined in late June, the Olympian Hiawatha is a curiosity to the passengers on the observation platform of the Columbian and to the rest of the far Northwest. Streamliners were late in coming to the Northwest (after World War II) and newspapers in Washington, Idaho, Montana and the Dakotas had editorialized for some years on the "slow train through the Ozarks" schedules of the three main line carriers to the Northwest. The one notable exception was the Union Pacific Portland Rose streamliner to Chicago via Omaha.

W. R. McGee

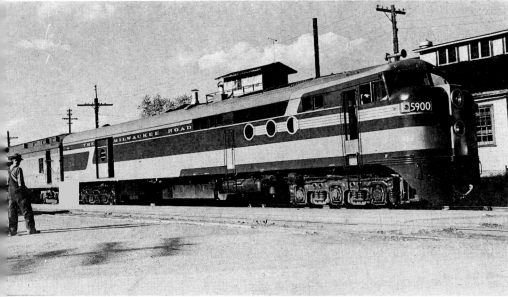

TWO OF THE MORE interesting pieces of equipment turned out by the Milwaukee Shops were "Diesel-Electric Motor Cars," 5900 and 5901, built in 1948 and powered by a 1,000 h.p. General Motors Diesel, model 12-567-A. Half baggage compartment, the 85' units, designed for light passenger service, and built to replace aging steam power, were capable of exerting 24,000 lbs. of tractive effort and had a top speed of 75 mph. With the forward truck only being powered, they were handicapped by slippery starting characteristics with any kind of a trailing load.
*Harold J. Davidson and
C. C. Tinkham*

WITH DRY SNOW blowing off the tops of the cars, and startled pigeons scattering to the four winds, train 58, the River Division Local, sweeps out of Minneapolis behind Erie built Fairbanks Morse power.
Jack Malven

TRAIN NO. 263, detouring over the Northern Pacific at Laurel, Montana, moves west behind three F7 units in March, 1951. Cut in behind the new F7's (delivered in 1950) is an air conditioned caboose — the private business car of one of the road officials.

W. R. McGee

AN SD-9 AND TWO SD-7's lead a Cedar Falls branch freight over the approach to the Skykomish River covered bridge near Monroe, Washington.
Stuart Hertz

THE DAY OF THE IRON HORSE is just about over. Oil burning Pacifics, Prairies, Mikes and Consolidations line the storage tracks at Othello in 1955. A few engines still serve as standby power, but with delivery of the new diesel units, even these few old locomotives will be towed to the scrap yard at Tacoma. The gap in the electrification between Othello and Avery will not be filled by steam, nor by electrics, but by locomotives that carry their own generating plants on board — the diesel electric.

Collection of Wally Swanson

THE EASTBOUND Olympian Hiawatha has just emerged from Snoqualmie Pass tunnel, and now curves past company houses and the sub station at Hyak, the summit of Snoqualmie Pass. In about a mile, the train will pass the site of the old Milwaukee Ski Bowl, the facility that did much to popularize Snoqualmie Pass as a winter sports recreation area. Although this photo was taken in late May of 1961, snow still lays heavily through much of the area. Accumulated snowfall approaching 200 inches is not uncommon here, explaining the ten foot high foundations on the company houses.

Robert E. Oestreich

NEAR THE WEST EDGE of Sparta, in the rolling hill country of Wisconsin, Extra 69 (thirty-eight cars) meets train 262 (one hundred thirty-one cars), powered by a trio of GP 40's and a GP 35.

Jim Scribbins

AT SAPPINGTON, Montana a fast moving seven car Olympian Hiawatha races past a one hundred car eastbound extra freight, "in the hole." On the parallel tracks of the Northern Pacific, on this May day in 1959, the westbound North Coast Limited was less than ten minutes away.

Philip C. Johnson

THREE E9 UNITS POWER THE Olympian Hiawatha of 1961 up Snoqualmie Pass and across the sharply curved trestle at Hanson's Creek, one of several such trestles on the west side of the pass. Passenger equipment was repainted in Union Pacific colors in 1956, after the Milwaukee contracted to forward the Union Pacific "City" streamliners between Chicago and Omaha. Some officers of the road felt that the Milwaukee lost much of its individuality when it gave up its traditional color scheme of orange, maroon and light gray.   *Robert E. Oestreich*

IN 1968, A SOLID TRAIN OF grain hoppers, powered by six diesel units, rolls steadily out onto Red Coulee Bridge, in daily use since its completion in 1913.

The Milwaukee Road

Chapter V
Meeting The Challenges
Bankruptcy — War — Regulation — Competition

As the Milwaukee moved into its westward expansion, the road was in excellent financial condition, but the combination of many events and circumstances, over the next few years was to reverse this solid position and eventually lead the road into bankruptcy. The cost of the westward extension had greatly exceeded the estimates. The Northern Pacific, (which cost nearly $70,000,000 to build in the 1880's) had received large land grants to aid in its construction, amounting to a staggering total of 44,000,000 acres, an area equal to the state of Missouri. By 1917, with most of this land still unsold, it reported gross receipts from land sales of over $136,000,000. The Great Northern had traded the Red River Valley of the North lands, the grant of a predecessor company, for even better heavily timbered sections further west. Without generous land grants, the Milwaukee was forced to negotiate for its right of way in a spiraling market, with land values inflated by speculators, and by the actions of its rivals. The Milwaukee also increased its costs, because most of the construction was of a permanent nature. Temporary construction, which could suffice for the time at less cost and be improved later, was largely avoided. In addition, the Milwaukee's labor costs were much higher than those of its rivals, who had built largely with cheap and exploited labor. As the Milwaukee pushed westward, the competition for labor created by the tremendous amount of railroad construction taking place throughout the country, pushed its price up.

Still it was not the cost of its westward expansion alone, that created trouble for the Milwaukee. Basically its operating expenses and bond interest exceeded its revenue, and there was an increase in the company's funded debt in the public hands. The business that was to pay for the western extension simply did not materialize. The building boom in the Pacific Northwest peeked about 1907, and the lumber industry stabilized about 1910. The competition from the other roads was formidable. The Great Northern covered the Northwest like a blanket, and the Union Pacific had pushed its tap roots into the Northwest from many points. The most formidable competition of all came from the Panama Canal when it was opened in 1914. More projected business was lost with the increase of automobiles, trucks and busses on public highways (encouraged by the Federal Aid Road Act of 1917). Added to the expenses of the road, already heavily in debt, were soaring taxes, increased cost of maintenance, improvements and additions to the line, and the Adamson Law which increased wages.

Matters were further complicated when the Federal Government took over the railroads during World War I. Harry E. Byram, who had become president of the road in 1917, made way for R. M. Calkins in 1918, and became the federal manager for the road until control was returned to the company in 1920, and he resumed the presidency. The government ran the roads at a loss and without proper maintenance or replacement of rolling stock, and a federal mortgage was placed on the company equipment in the form of equipment trust notes.

As if the road didn't have enough debt of its own, it acquired a lease on the Chicago, Terre Haute & Southeastern Railway Company that lead to the coal fields of Southern Indiana, and in 1922,

IN THE LATE 1920's and early 1930's, the Milwaukee operated many branchline passenger operations in the far West, such as the Everett-Cedar Falls local, shown here in Everett in the 1920's. As roads improved, these local runs were abandoned due to lack of business and increased competition from bus lines and private automobiles.

Pringle & Richards Studio

acquired the Chicago Milwaukee & Gary to obtain a direct line to the former. The Milwaukee took over the heavy debts of both lines, and found that they were never able to operate them at a profit. Added to the road's problems were a coal strike, a shop strike in September, 1922, an ordered reduction in freight rates, a brief depression in some of the territory served by the road, and the liquidation of holdings by three of the four major stockholders. Also Kuhn Loeb & Company profited handsomely at the Railroad's expense in selling bond issues. Since the death of Miller in 1913, there had been no one capable of handling the large financial transactions.

Unable to reduce interest and operating expense or to increase revenue, the directors voted to go into receivership, March 17, 1925. Kuhn Loeb & Company and National City Bank became reorganization managers for the road, and in April, 1926 the road was up for sale and reorganization. The road's bankers came into control November 22, 1926 for $140,000,000 as the only bidders at the sale in Butte, Montana. On March 31, 1927, it was reorganized as the Chicago Milwaukee St. Paul & Pacific Railroad Company with Henry A. Scandrett (resigned as vice-president of the Union Pacific) as the new president and Byram as Chairman of the Board.

The road launched into a program of improvement of the property of the road, and inaugurated the use of roller-bearing trains. The Pioneer Limited, in 1927, was the first Milwaukee passenger train so equipped, followed closely by the Olympian and the Arrow. Hopes that the reorganization would return the road to a sound financial basis were not realized when the depression struck in 1929, hitting all the railroads hard. State and local taxes made heavy inroads on the income of the road in contrast to the public support of the highways for trucking. There was a continual loss of revenue due to Interstate Commerce Commission decisions on rates, and declining passenger business. In 1920, the road had carried 16,000,000 passengers, in 1930, only 6,700,000. There was a brief increase of revenue due to traffic carried for the Chicago World's Fair, but in the years between 1921 and 1940, only three were concluded without a deficit.

On June 29, 1935, the road again declared bankruptcy, but the reorganization was to be delayed through the courts for another ten years. In the meantime, the road continued to operate under a trusteeship. The Milwaukee decided that speed was the means to compete with highway traffic, which had continued to grow with the mass production of cars, first launched by the production of Henry Ford's model T in 1908. On July 20, 1934, the road had established a new world's sustained speed record for passenger trains. On a test run from Chicago to Milwaukee, a roller-bearing equipped five car

163

THE MAIL AND HEAD END CREW OF THIS Milwaukee passenger train were probably photographed around the time of the first World War, when wooden equipment was still widely used.

Edward W. Nolan

steel train, averaged 92.62 mph on the 61.4 miles between Edgewood, Ill. and Oakwood, Wis. Such sustained speed was costly and there were dangers involving crossings, but work continued on the development of high speed trains. The first streamliner, the Hiawatha, was put into service on May 29, 1935, between Chicago and St. Paul, covering the 410 miles in 6½ hours. This 100 mph speed, in the days of the development of the propeller driven aircraft, and when 60 mph for cars was considered fast, was greeted most enthusiastically by the public. Its success led to a Morning Hiawatha and an Afternoon Hiawatha. By 1940, a Midwest Hiawatha ran between Chicago, Omaha, Sioux City and Sioux Falls, and by 1947, the Olympian Hiawatha covered the run between Chicago and Seattle.

The Milwaukee Shops continued to play an important role under the direction of Karl F. Nystrom, who held over one hundred personal patents, and was largely responsible for the development of the Hiawatha. The first welded steel passenger cars for the Hiawatha were built in 1934, and in 1938, the Milwaukee was the first railroad to eliminate elliptic springs in passenger car trucks, replacing them with helical springs like those used in freight cars.

As a public service, the Milwaukee helped to promote and advance water conservation and irrigation development projects in all of the northwestern states, and in the winter of 1937-1938, in cooperation with the Seattle Times, helped to devel-

op and promote the Milwaukee Ski Bowl, at Snoqualmie Pass. Located on Milwaukee property at the top of the Pass between the east portal of Snoqualmie tunnel and Hyak, the Ski Bowl lay in a natural bowl formed by the Cascade Mountains, and featured five ski runs named for crack Milwaukee trains — Hiawatha, Chippewa, Arrow, Pioneer and Olympian. The Seattle Times sponsored ski school classes at no charge for all who wished to participate, but primarily for youngsters at school, and the Milwaukee provided safe transportation at reasonable rates. Ski trains operated on a two hour schedule every Saturday and Sunday over the sixty-one miles from Seattle (where it was estimated there were 95,000 ski enthusiasts) and the slightly greater distance of 81 miles from Tacoma, in a lot less time than it was possible to drive it.

Popularity of the Bowl grew, and where originally it was estimated that only about 300 patrons at a time would be using the facilities, in the first year of operation, daily patronage averaged about 1,000, and it was necessary to bring in extra coaches for the ski trains from all over the system during the winter season and to operate the trains in several sections. No overnight accommodations were available, but there was a good ski lodge, expanded several times, where meals were served, and night skiing was started with trains leaving Seattle at six and returning about midnight, allowing about 2½ hours of skiing. In December, 1949, a disastrous fire destroyed the lodge with a loss of nearly a quarter million dollars. The plan to rebuild and continue to operate the ski trains was abandoned, because of the rapidly rising cost of operating the trains, and because of the growing popularity of other ski areas now easily accessible by automobile on nearby Snoqualmie Pass Highway 10.

The war in Europe and the Transportation Act in 1940, which among other things established payment by the government of the full tariff for transporting non-military personnel and property, brought a period of prosperity to the railroads. With the entry of the United States into World War II, the railroads did a fantastic job of carrying a tremendous load in troops, materials and supplies in spite of the loss of experienced personnel to the armed forces, and a shortage of equipment. Increased revenue was derived from the halting of commercial shipments through the Panama Canal and the shifting of them to the railroads, and from the establishment of widely scattered ordinance plants, the most notable achievement for the Milwaukee being the Atomic Energy Plant at Hanford, Washington. The government seized control of the railroads for a very brief period between December 27, 1943 and January 18, 1944 when the threat of a strike loomed.

On February 23, 1945, the court confirmed the reorganization plan, ending ten years of receivership, and the road continued expanding and improving under the same management. The prosperity of the post war era was brief. By 1946, revenues were again dropping, costs were increasing and passenger service declining. In an attempt to attract passenger business, the road offered a credit card plan and worked out a cooperative agreement with Hertz car rentals.

In 1947, Charles H. Buford, an Arkansan, who had been with the road since 1907, became president. There was now the beginning of a changing attitude on the part of the government and the newspapers toward the railroads. The fallacy of continuing to use the railroads as a whipping boy was becoming evident. The railroads, which had borne the cost of their construction, were heavily taxed, while competing forms of transportation, the waterways, the highways and finally the airlines, built with tax funds, were subsidized. Such unequal treatment could only result in the railroads running down and eventually going broke, yet the war, if nothing else, had pointed out just how vital the railroads were to the country. If they were allowed to go under, they would have to be rehabilitated at public expense. Unfortunately, realizing that a problem exists is only the first step toward solving it, and action has been far slower than words.

In 1950, the Milwaukee celebrated its centennial, and soon began a program of rebuilding and modernizing its freight yards. By 1955, the Milwaukee had taken over the operation of the Union Pacific's famous "Cities" trains between Chicago and Omaha — The City of Los Angeles, City of San Francisco, City of Denver, City of Portland and the coach train, the Challenger. In the same year, the last regularly scheduled steam locomotive was run, although a few steam locomotives were kept on standby and the last run actually was made March 16, 1957.

MILWAUKEE ROAD NO. 41, Class H8 American type, at Des Plaines, Illinois in 1939, was one of a group of 4-4-0's (Milwaukee Numbers 35-98), that were acquired when the Milwaukee Road purchased the Chicago Terre Haute & South Eastern Railroad. Modern appearing locomotives for an American type, the engines were widely used on lightly traveled branch lines throughout the Milwaukee system. Many of the class were still in service through World War II, and final disposition was made in 1951, when the last of them was scrapped.

Collection of H. K. Vollrath

THE COLUMBIAN OF THE 1920's passes the source of the Missouri River — the junction of the Jefferson, Madison and Gallatin Rivers in Montana.

The Milwaukee Road

John P. Kiley, who had first joined the road in 1913, succeeded Charles H. Buford as president of the Milwaukee on September 1, 1950. Upon his retirement December 31, 1957, he was succeeded by William J. Quinn, who in 1954, had joined the road's law department and had served as general solicitor, vice-president, and general council. Mr. Quinn served as president of the Milwaukee for five years before moving on to become the president of the Chicago Burlington & Quincy, and was succeeded in turn by Curtiss E. Crippen.

By 1962, the family car was carrying about 90% of the intercity passenger traffic, as compared to 58% in 1944. The intercity freight traffic carried by rail, dropped from 70% of the total in 1944, to only 41% by 1962. Net income for the railroads fell by 58%, and employment was cut by one third. The industry fought to reverse the trend with new ideas. In 1958, the Milwaukee began its piggyback operations, and in 1959, installed the Carscope car tracing system to provide up-to-the-minute data on freight car movements.

Late in 1938, a reorganization plan with a proposed merger between the Chicago Milwaukee St. Paul and Pacific and the Chicago & North Western had been turned down. In 1960, new talks concerning consolidation were under way. A $1,000,000 "one spot car repair" facility went into operation at the Bensenville freight yard, and tri-level freight cars were put into service to carry motor vehicles. Modernized, double-deck, air conditioned commuter coaches were put into service on the Milwaukee's suburban operation in Chicago in 1961, and with continued growth in the volume of traffic, six former road passenger coaches were converted for use on the commuter trains in 1968. By 1961, the data processing installation, begun the year before at the Fullerton Avenue accounting offices in Chicago, was complete and in operation. This installation, in turn, was completely replaced in 1968, by two new third generation computer systems to process accounting, sales analyses, inventory control and other functions. In 1962, the railroad expanded both its use of VHF radio for communication and its automatic dialing system for the company's own phone lines, and installed the first hot box detectors.

The XL Special and Thunderhawk freights, cutting a full day off previous schedules between Chicago and the Pacific Northwest, began running, and the first link of a microwave relay communications system was installed, in 1963. A major freight car rebuilding program was started, and the first

THE SACAJAWEA HOTEL AT Three Forks, Montana, built by the railroad in the early 1920's was named for the Indian woman who served as a guide to the Lewis and Clark expedition through this same area in 1805 and 1806.
The Milwaukee Road

THE MILWAUKEE ROAD - SKI BOWL -

TALLEY-HO SKIBOGGAN

STUDENT SKI JUMP

SKI LODGE

ROCKY POINT

NEW SKIBOGGAN LIFT - 4 ROPE TOWS -
GREATLY ENLARGED AREA

Giant Hill Jumps Designed By Hostmark

The Ski Jumps were designed by Peter Hostmark, a national authority on ski jumping, and these jumping hills are considered among the finest in the world. It was on this big hill in 1941 that the late Torger Tokle leaped to an American record jump of 288 feet. Tokle gallantly gave his life serving with the United States Ski Troops in Italy during World War II.

The Seattle Times will sponsor, for the first time, jumping school under the direction of Olav Ulland and auspices of the Seattle Ski Club, and these jumping classes will be held each Sunday commencing December 29.

Olympic Trials Scheduled For Ski Bowl

This season, on March 22nd and 23rd, The Milwaukee Road Ski Bowl will be the scene of the United States Olympic Team Ski Jumping Trials being sponsored by the Seattle Ski Club. This great event will bring to the Ski Bowl the finest jumpers in the United States besides a great jumping team from Norway.

A Big Comfortable Lodge in The Heart of the Cascades

Luxurious alpine lodge, offering comfortable dining room facilities, fireplace, rumpus room, ski shop, modern plumbing, makes it the outstanding ski headquarters in the Northwest. On the second floor of the left wing of the lodge is a huge lounging room with an open fireplace, easy chairs, card tables, and a dance floor. In the right wing is the cafeteria restaurant. Downstairs there is an adequate checking room for extra equipment. Comfortable rest rooms are provided for men and women. There is an up-to-date waxing room complete with steam tables for warming skis prior to waxing, and electric plates and irons for applying base wax. The entire lodge is kept warm and comfortable by central heating and supplements the open fireplace.

The Ski Jumps are just above and in front of the Lodge, and one may enjoy this thrilling sport from the porch or windows of the Lodge, without the discomfort of a long, tiring hike through the snow.

•

(There will be no overnight accommodations, and the former policy will be continued which provides for no liquor or gambling permitted on the trains, on the grounds, or in the Lodge.)

SPECIAL NIGHT TRAINS

The Milwaukee Road will again feature NIGHT SNOW TRAINS under special arrangements by clubs and other groups on a minimum basis of a 250-passenger guarantee, and such train schedules will be adjusted to the wishes of the groups that desire to sponsor these trains.

Don't stay home . . . enjoy yourself at The Milwaukee Road Ski Bowl, the Northwest's greatest ski paradise. Only two hours by train in warm, comfortable coaches, and convenient running schedule from Tacoma and valley towns. The train schedules are planned to give you an enjoyable day on the snow fields. Special arrangements for private parties may be made by applying to your nearest Milwaukee Road Ticket Office. Remember, there is no worrying about road or traffic conditions when you travel by train. It is fun to ski by rail.

THE FIRST SECTION OF A SKI train completes unloading at the Milwaukee Ski Bowl, as a second section pulls in from Tacoma. After the engines have run around the coaches and coupled to the opposite ends, both trains will lay over until late afternoon for the return trip. Although steam power was authorized for power on ski trains if the occasion should require, with a turn around at Easton, Washington, it was never used, and probably would have had to come from Othello, as no steam passenger power was regularly assigned to Seattle/Tacoma.

Collection of Ed Notske

unit train operation carried coal from the mines to an Indiana power generating plant. The following year the first grain unit trains were put into service, and a gantry crane installed at Bensenville to facilitate the piggyback operations. A new contemporary design passenger station opened in Milwaukee in 1965, and in 1966, the first all-piggy-back-train to operate between Chicago and the Twin Cities was run.

Carscope, the Milwaukee Road's car information center, located in the Transportation Department in Chicago, installed a 360 computer system in 1967, which gave virtually instantaneous access to information on freight car location. Later the 360 was equipped with the first video display units to be used by a Midwest railroad. This system was replaced in 1969, by an even more highly sophisticated computer system, with four times the storage and processing capacity, and establishing automatic direct communications between the Carscope computer and field locations.

170

THE MILWAUKEE SKI Bowl was first known as the Snoqualmie Ski Bowl, but in order to avoid confusion with other ski areas at the top of Snoqualmie Pass, the name was changed in 1946, when the Bowl was re-opened after its closure during World War II. The Milwaukee Ski Bowl was not only famous for the ski schools held there, but also as the site of the National Ski Jumping Championships in 1941 when Torger Tokle set a new jump record of 288'.

Collection of Ed Notske

ACTION PHOTOS of meets between Bi-polars and any other electric locomotive on the Milwaukee main line in the Cascades and Saddle Mountains of Washington are rare, largely because of the inaccessibility of the areas and the light traffic. Here freight motor E-30 on a westbound freight at Hyak in 1939 waits "in the hole" for the second section of a ski train to pull clear of the siding switch, before it takes the main and proceeds down Snoqualmie Pass.

Collection of Don Dietrich

SKI INSTRUCTOR, Ed Notske, demonstrates a "snowplow" turn to a beginning class at Milwaukee Ski Bowl, against a backdrop of mountains, firs, and day coaches spotted for reloading at the end of the skiing day.

The Seattle Times

A TWELVE CAR SKI train climbs the long grade up Snoqualmie Pass from Cedar Falls to Hyak. Cut into the consist are two modern dining cars off the Olympian, for use by Seattle Times newspaper carriers on a special outing to the ski bowl. The usual ski train was made up of elderly, red plush coaches, complete with stained glass upper sash, and some were even equipped with coal burning stoves. A baggage car, for the equipment, was cut in behind the locomotive, and another baggage car with a juke box for dancing, was located about the middle of the ten to twelve car train.

Jack Anderson

Land transactions and the locating of new industries on sites served by the Milwaukee, continued to be an important part of the company's activities. A principal land acquisition by the Milwaukee in 1968, was the one hundred twenty acre site at Kent, Washington for future railroad development.

Capital improvements continued in 1968, with the acquisition of about five hundred new freight cars and twenty-five new diesel locomotives. The increase of shipments of motor vehicles also made it necessary to add to the already large fleet of multi-level rack cars. Under a freight car rebuilding program, 627 cars were put into like new condition and improvements were made to 920 others. Improvements designed to upgrade the service characteristics of diesel locomotives, and to increase their versatility, were also implemented. In Tacoma, a 123' by 500' modern car repair shop replaced the existing structure. With the rapid growth of the piggyback operation, including the handling of containers, facilities were redesigned, upgraded and enlarged at St. Paul, Chicago, Sioux City and Seattle.

Because of the steadily rising volume of traffic moving over the railroad to or from Pacific North Coast ports and the Orient, especially Japan, the road opened the Milwaukee Road freight sales office in Tokyo March 1, 1968. The effort by the various ports to construct special piers and to install cranes, greatly increased the number of ships and volume of cargo. Most American and Japanese line container vessels, now calling at Pacific North Coast ports, discharge containers for Milwaukee Road handling to the Midwest, and points beyond via connecting carriers. Later in the year, the Milwaukee, having been an intermediate carrier in "land bridge rates," established by other origin and destination railroads, issued its own rates for the movement of the containers between the ports of Longview, Seattle and Tacoma, Washington, and also between the eastern seaboard ports on traffic originating and terminating in foreign countries.

Progress toward and preparation for a merger with the Chicago and North Western continued all through the 1960's. By December 1968, the prospects of the merger seemed assured with the favorable report of the Interstate Commerce Commission. Exceptions to the report were to be filed by interested parties no later than March 31, 1969, giving rise to the hope that the decision would be made before the end of the year. However, a split and price drop on Chicago and North Western stock brought about the resistance of Milwaukee stock holders, and the merger did not take place.

Another merger was to have significant effect upon the activities of the Milwaukee — the merger of the Great Northern, the Northern Pacific, and the Chicago Burlington & Quincy — to become the Burlington Northern. The merger was approved March 3, 1970, subject to certain conditions in favor of the Milwaukee. The Milwaukee gained access into Portland via Longview Junction and trackage rights over the Burlington Northern, and obtained trackage rights north of Seattle giving the Milwaukee an interchange with the Canadian Pacific Railroad at Sumas. Access to Billings, Montana was acquired through a car handling arrangement with the Northern Lines. A change was made in the basis of switching rates in the territory west of the Twin Cities, and the opening of eleven gateways in North Dakota, Montana, and Washington, enabled the Milwaukee to compete for the long haul traffic which it had formerly been compelled to surrender to or receive from the Northern Lines at the Twin Cities.

Passenger service decline, over the years, made it necessary to discontinue some operations. The Olympian Hiawatha had made its last run from Seattle on May 22, 1961. The inauguration of Amtrak on May 1, 1971, with few exceptions, removed the railroads from the passenger business, and the Milwaukee now forwards the Empire Builder between Chicago and the Twin Cities for Amtrak. The flashing Hiawathas have followed the Olympian Hiawatha into oblivion, and only the memory of the orange and maroon streamliners and limiteds remains. Still, out of Harlowton, the freights move east and west behind orange and black units bearing the proud slanted herald of the Milwaukee Road. Little Joes move over the high passes of the Rockies, the Belts, and the Bitter Roots. Out of Avery, an old GE box-cab locks couplers behind the caboose of a through freight to help in the daily conquering of St. Paul Pass. GE and Alco built freighters whine down the long pass over the Cascades, and mile long freights grind up the 2.2% grade from the Columbia. Air horns have replaced peanut whistles in the Cascades, but the steel wheels are still rolling on the rails in the Northwest, and the familiar orange of the Milwaukee is a daily sight from the Midwest to the Pacific Coast.

172

ONE OF THE BEST KEPT secrets of World War II was the building of the atomic reactor at Hanford, Washington, and the production of the fissionable material for the A-bombs used on Hiroshima and Nagasaki in 1945. Even the railroad crews that worked the Hanford branch with 100 car freights from Beverly Junction on the Columbia River to the dusty little tank town of Hanford — that prior to the building of the reactor barely warranted one car a day — even suspected what was actually going on. One reason the secret was well kept was that the crews were never actually allowed inside what had become a U.S. military reservation. The secret buildings were miles inside of the desert reservation, and the government took over the railroad at Hanford, with military crews only handling the trains from Hanford south to the sites. Shown here is the once a day local at Hanford in 1939, with the Columbia River in the background.

W. R. McGee

A TROOP TRAIN, RUNNING as the first section of No. 15, the Olympian, pauses for a lengthy stop at Three Forks, Montana, and servicemen pile off the train to head for the USO snack bar, or to make a wild dash downtown in search of more spirited refreshment. The express boxcar, behind the locomotive, is perhaps the most modern car in the entire train — the coaches (red plush) dating back to at least the first World War, and the Pullmans not a great deal newer. A trip from Chicago to Seattle in the day coaches was a memorable experience, with sleep almost impossible, and a somewhat comatose state was the best way to make the long trip.

W. R. McGee

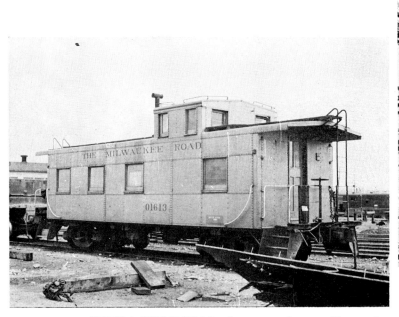

CUPOLA STYLE ROAD cabooses are shown at Tacoma in 1958. Steel caboose No. 01613 was painted orange with maroon lettering. Wooden caboose No. 01020 (since scrapped) was painted dull red with white lettering.

L. C. Bellows

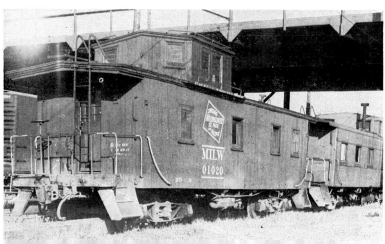

THE OLD COLUMBIAN, TRAIN 18, was revived to operate on the slower schedule of the old Olympian, when the new, fast Olympian Hiawatha went into service. Like its running mates on the Great Northern and Northern Pacific, the Columbian carried an assorted mix of lightweight and standard weight equipment, and a number of head end cars were used to carry storage mail and express. Serving a lightly populated area, and lacking a mail contract to help pay the overhead, the Columbian did not last long, and was removed from the schedule during the mid 1950's.

W. R. McGee

THE WINTER OF 1947 was particularly severe in the Midwest, and the Milwaukee was hit hard by heavy snow and sub zero temperatures, that stalled and delayed traffic. On the first of February, a work train extra called to plow out drifts and clear switches, pauses at Ripon, Wisconsin.

Collection of Don Dietrich

THE OLD TACOMA & EASTERN station in Tacoma, long used by the Milwaukee, was sold when a new passenger facility was completed on Milwaukee Way parallel to the Tacoma freight yard.

Stuart Hertz

MILWAUKEE TERMINAL caboose No. 01372 is built on the cast steel underframe of a scrapped steam locomotive tender. Fitted with oil stoves, seats and toilet facilities, the terminal cabooses are in service in some of the larger yards on the road.

The Milwaukee Road

THE OLD TWO TONE GRAY Milwaukee Road way station at Kittitas, Washington, located just east of Ellensburg near the west slope of the Saddle Mountains, is typical of small stations throughout the West. The generating plant in the background feeds the catenary for the electric operation east and west of this point. April, 1971

Robert E. Oestreich

EXCEPT FOR THE modern handset city telephone, the operator's desk and company equipment in the Kittitas station is essentially the same as it was when the station was built in 1908.

Robert E. Oestreich

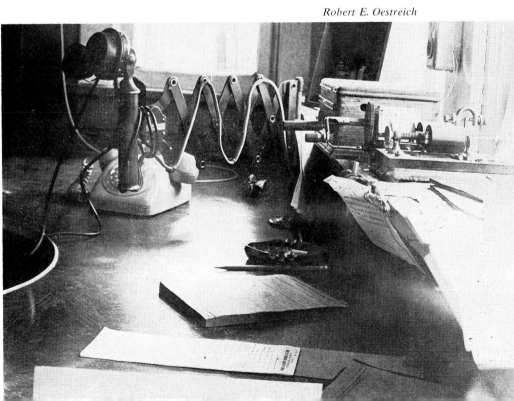

WITH THREE MAIL STORAGE cars on the head end, and minus the Skytop Lounge observation car on the rear, the Olympian Hiawatha has made its last run into Union Station, Seattle, May 24, 1961. The last eastbound train had departed two days earlier for Chicago, ending a half century of Milwaukee Road passenger service to the Pacific Coast.

Robert E. Oestreich

SNOW COVERED MT. RAINIER serves as the backdrop to the action as a GP-7 leads two E-8 units across Northern Pacific-Great Northern high iron near Black River Junction in April of 1960. The GP-7 on the point of the Olympian Hiawatha will change positions with the trailing E-8 cab unit when the locomotive runs around the train at Union Station, but the GP-7 is given the honor of leading the varnish from Tacoma into Seattle.

Robert E. Oestreich

UNION STATION IN SEATTLE, BUILT by the OWR & N (Union Pacific) in 1911, is shown on the last day that it was open for operation, April 30, 1971. The Milwaukee Road shared the station with the Union Pacific, as a tenant, prior to the termination of the Olympian Hiawatha in May of 1961. A magnificent edifice by any standards, Union Station was regarded by many as having the most imposing interior of any station in the Pacific Northwest.

Robert E. Oestreich

181

A SMALL GROUP OF PASSENGERS waits to board the eastbound Olympian Hiawatha at Missoula, in 1958. The imposing station is still being used by the road, in 1971, although passenger service has been gone for the past decade. The Clark Fork (of the Columbia River) flows beside the tracks and through the heart of Missoula. On its opposite bank, run the rails of the Northern Pacific.

Philip C. Johnson

AN E-8 IN UNION PACIFIC COLORS of yellow, red and gray, heads the eastbound Olympian Hiawatha down the main in Maple Valley in May of 1961. Soon to be discontinued, the sight of the streamliner on its daily run would be missed by many, as were the magnificent Bi-polars that had left the Coast Division several years before.

Robert E. Oestreich

AT THE ICING FACILITY IN the Milwaukee Road yard at Othello, Washington, the ice for the reefers is crushed and salted to order by the little electric powered crusher, running on rails on top of the icing dock. Steam power switches the reefers to the dock, but one electrified track passes to the left of the dock, and main line freights pass by to the far right behind electric locomotives.

The Milwaukee Road

NEW AUTOMOBILES AND TRUCKS are shown arriving at the Milwaukee Road's automobile marshaling complex at Kent, Washington. The yard is the largest and most modern of its kind in the Pacific Northwest. The automobiles pictured here are being unloaded from tri-level automobile rack cars in the area operated by Convoy Company of Portland, Ore.

The Milwaukee Road

MILWAUKEE GOLDEN GRAIN TRAIN — forty cars of Montana wheat — was loaded in the Great Falls area and shipped as a unit train to Longview, Washington for loading aboard ship to the Orient.

The Milwaukee Road

TWO GENERAL ELECTRIC U-BOATS move slowly by the Tacoma sub-station in April, 1971 with a trainload of logs destined for the Tacoma mills.

Robert E. Oestreich

AN OPEN TOP WOODCHIP CAR, one of 150 specially built under the Milwaukee Road's 1969 capital improvement program, is shown ready to load at a western Washington chip mill. The steel cars are 63¾ feet long and have a 100 ton capacity.

The Milwaukee Road

LEAD MOTORS OF AN EASTBOUND freight pass over State Highway No. 7c at Beverly, Washington, in 1966, after crossing the mighty Columbia River. At Othello, thirty-eight miles ahead, the motors will give way to the diesels used to cross the non-electrified gap between Othello and Avery, Idaho.

Robert E. Oestreich

A MILWAUKEE ROAD UNIT TRAIN which hauls coal from an Indiana Mine to a power plant near Terre Haute, crosses the Wabash River in 1967. Trailing is one of the newest bay window type caboose built in 1956/57.

The Milwaukee Road

CROSSING THE COLUMBIA at Beverly, Washington, a mile long eastbound freight responds to the pull, tug and push of 19,000 hp. The four electric and two diesel units on the head end are assisted by four electrics in the middle, to equalize the strain on the drawbars. Auto racks and a bay window caboose bring up the rear markers.

Robert E. Oestreich

LOADING AND UNLOADING OF PIGGYBACK trailers in the Seattle yard is accomplished by an FWD "Piggy Packer" modified for better handling and increased capacity by the Milwaukee shops.

The Milwaukee Road

A PAIR OF GE U-BOATS lead the first through freight into the Burlington Northern yards at Portland, Oregon on March 22, 1971. Prior to this date, all Milwaukee trains southbound from Seattle, had terminated some fifty miles from Portland, at Longview Junction. The Milwaukee business car behind the diesels carries officials of the road to a meeting with members of the Portland Chamber of Commerce and a celebration honoring the occasion.

The Milwaukee Road

Bibliography

BOOKS

Abdill, George, B. This was Railroading. Superior Publishing Co. 1958

Beebe, Lucius, and Clegg, Charles. The Trains We Rode. Vol. 1. Howell-North. 1965

Brain, Insley, J. Jr. The Milwaukee Road Electrification. Bay Area Electric Assn. 1961

Derleth, August. The Milwaukee Road. Stratford Press, Inc. 1948

Donovan, Frank, P. The Milwaukee in Iowa. State Historical Society of Iowa. May 1964

Droege, John A. Passenger Terminals and Trains. Kalmbach. 1969

Farrington, S. Kip, Jr. Railroads at War. Coward McCann. 1944

----. Railroading from the Rear End. Coward McCann. 1946

----. Railroading from the Head End. Doubleday Boran & Co. 1943

Holbrook, Stewart H. Story of American Railroads. Crown Publishing. 1947

----. James J. Hill. Knopf Publishing Co. 1955

Jacobs, David. Bridges Tunnels and Canals. American Heritage Publishing Co. 1968

Locomotive Cyclopedia of American Practice. Simmons-Boardman Publishing Co. 1944

Long, Lunan H. The World Almanac, 1970. Doubleday and Co.

Morrison, Samuel H. and Commanger, Henry, Steele. The Growth of the American Republic. Oxford University Press. 1940

Morgan, David P. Steams Finest Hour. Kalmbach. 1959

Salisbury, Albert and Jane. Two Captains West. Superior Publishing Co. 1950

Warner, Paul T. Locomotives of the Milwaukee Road. Vol. 2. Southern California Chapter Railway and Locomotive Historical Society. 1958

Westcott, Linn H. Cyclopedia Steam Locomotives, Vol. 1. Kalmbach. 1960

Westing, Fred. The Locomotives Baldwin Built. Superior Publishing Co. 1966

Wheeler, Olin D. Wonderland 1903. Chas. S. Fee

TECHNICAL PAMPHLETS AND BOOKLETS

Locomotive Data. Baldwin Locomotive Works. 1921

Operating Instructions for Electric Freight Locomotives. Milwaukee Road. 1950

Progress in Steam Railway Electrification. General Electric Co. 1922

The Electric Division of the Chicago Milwaukee and St. Paul Railway. General Electric Co. 1925

Railroad Electrification Data. Westinghouse Electric and Manufacturing Co. 1926

TIMETABLES

Milwaukee Road. 1912. 1925. 1928. 1946. 1948.

Operating Timetables for Employees. Milwaukee Road. 1946. 1948

NEWSPAPERS

Butte Miner

Montana Standard

Seattle Post-Intelligencer

Seattle Daily Times

Spokane Chronicle

Spokesman Review

Wall Street Journal

MAGAZINES

Milwaukee Employees

Model Railroader

Railroad Magazine

Trains. Kalmbach Publishing Company, Milwaukee, Wisc., July 1963. Rogers, Gordon W. Butte Anaconda & Pacific

The Potlatch Story

Chicago, Milwaukee & St. Paul Railway.

Chicago—Milwaukee—St. Paul—Minneapolis Aberdeen—Butte—Seattle—Tacoma.

Continued from pages 23 and 24. 8-18-12

Table 13 — Central Time

17	3	15	1	Mls.	H. & D. Division	Elevation	6	18	4	16
PM	PM	AM	AM				AM	AM	PM	PM
*1025	*5.15	*1100	*7.45	410.1	Lv...St. Paul...Ar	704	8.05	9.30	7.10	10.50
	5.30		8.00	415.3	«...Merriam Park...«	810	7.50		6.55	
11.10	6.00	11.45	8.30	420.1	«..Minneapolis..«	826	7.20	8.45	6.20	10.05
	◉			421.9	«..So. Minneapolis..«	842		◆		
	6.16	◉	8.45	424.0	«...Nicollet Ave...«	872	6.58	◆	5.55	◆
	◉	◉	8.56	428.1	«..St. Louis Park..«	917		◆	5.43	◆
	6.30	◉	9.01	430.5	«...Hopkins...Lv	920	6.43	◆	5.38	◆
	6.44	◉	9.16	438.4	«...Chanhassen...«	962	6.31	◆	5.23	◆
	◉		s9.33	447.2	«..Augusta..«	978		◆	s5.07	◆
				450.8	«..Benton Jct..«	942				
	7.15	◉	9.46	452.7	«..Cologne..«	944	6.04	◆	4.56	◆
	◉		s9.53	456.1	«..Bongards..«	978		◆	4.40	◆
	7 28	◉	10.03	460.0	«..Norwood..«	987	5.45	◆	4.32	◆
	7.39	◉	10.13	465.5	«..Plato..«	993	s5.35	◆	4.20	◆
12.48	7 57	1 20	10.26	471.3	«..Glencoe..«	1001	5.25	7.09	4.10	8 27
	8 17	◉	10.37	477.1	«..Sumter..«	1030	s5.05	◆	3.50	◆
	8.33	◉	10.47	481.5	«..Brownton..«	1018	4.57	◆	3.40	◆
	8.47	◉	11.01	488.2	«..Stewart..«	1058	4.45	◆	3.26	◆
	9 02	◉	11.14	494.6	«..Buffalo Lake..«	1069	4.31	◆	3.10	◆
	9.13	◉	11.26	499.6	«..Hector..«	1076	4.21	◆	2.58	◆
	9 32	◉	11.44	508.6	«..Bird Island..«	1083	4.06	◆	2.35	◆
	9.43	◉	11.53	513.2	«..Olivia..«	1076	3.55	◆	2.15	◆
	9.55	◉	12.03	518.7	«..Danube..«	1076	s3.44	◆	2.02	◆
	10.07	◉	12.15	524.4	«..Renville..«	1059	3.34	◆	1.51	◆
	10.19	◉	12 27	531.3	«..Sacred Heart..«	1056	3.20	◆	1.38	◆
			s12.37	538.5	«..Minnesota Falls..«	1016		◆	s1.27	◆
	10.36	◉	12.46	540.5	«..Granite Falls..«	935	3.00	◆	1.18	◆
	s1055	◉	1.00	548.5	«..Wegdahl..«	927		◆	1.00	◆
3.00	11.10	3 13	‖1.10	553.9	Ar {Montevideo} Lv	922	2.32	5.00	12.50	6 27
3.10	11.20	3 20	1.25		Lv {Montevideo} Ar		2.20	4.55	‖1230	6.20
	s1135	◉	1.36	560.2	«..Watson...Lv	949	2.08	◆	12.15	◆
	11.51	◉	1 51	569.2	«..Milan..«	989	s1.54	◆	11.57	◆
3.47	12 07	3.57	2.06	577.4	«..Appleton..«	1001	1.40	◆	11.42	◆
	12.22	◉	2.18	584.2	«..Correll..«	974	s1.24	◆	11.27	◆
	12.39	◉	2.32	592.7	«..Odessa..«	957	1.10	◆	11.12	◆
	1.03	◉	2.48	599.2	«..Ortonville..«	985	12.40	◆	10.58	◆
4.22	1.33	◉	2.57	600.5	«Bigstone City, Minn«	970	12.28	b3.37	10.48	◆
				605.8	«Nubia, S.D..«	1068				
4.46	2.08	4.55	3 22	611.2	«..Milbank..«	1142	12.07	3.20	10.30	4 55
	2.23	◉	3.33	618.4	«..Twin Brooks..«	1258	11.47	◆	10.13	◆
	2.49	◉	3.51	626.3	«..Marvin..«	1651	11.31	◆	9.58	◆
	3.12	◉	4.13	633.6	«..Summit..«	1998	11.16	◆	9.43	◆
	s3.27	◉	4.28	642.0	«..Ortley..«	1862	s1059	◆	9.25	◆
	3.38	6.19	4.38	647.0	«..Waubay..«	1811	10.49	2.15	9.15	◆
	3.59	◉	4.57	657.5	«..Webster..«	1841	10.25	◆	8.55	3.25
6.08	s4.12	◉	5 08	664.0	«..Holmquist..«	1804	s1011	◆	8.40	◆
	4.24	◉	5 18	668.9	«..Bristol..«	1773	10.01	◆	8.30	◆
	4.45	◉ c	5.38	678.9	«..Andover..«	1473	9.35	◆	8.05	◆
	5.05	◉ c	5.58	688.6	«..Groton..«	1302	9.10	◆	7.40	2.26
	◉		6.10	694.4	«..James..«	1300		◆	7.26	◆
	s5.25	◉	6.20	699.7	«..Bath..«	1299	8.45	◆	7.14	◆
7.30	5.45	8.12	6.35	707.7	Ar {Aberdeen} Lv	1299	8.30	12.40	*6.50	1.55
7.45	6.15	8.25	PM		Lv {Aberdeen} Ar	1299	6.30	12.30	AM	1.40
	◉	◉		715.5	«..Fife...Lv	1381		d		
	6.42	◉		720.8	«..Mina..«	1432	6.02	d		
	s7.00	◉		728.8	«..Craven..«	1486	s5.46	d		
	7.15	9.04		734.0	«..Ipswich..«	1532	5.35	d		
	s7.31	◉		744.5	«..Beebe..«	1738	s5.19	d		
	7.54	◉		749.3	«..Roscoe..«	1826	5.05	a1121		
	s8.09	◉		755.9	«..Gretna..«	1916	s4.40	d		
9.22	8.29	◉		764.5	«..Bowdle...Lv	1993	4.20	10.55		
	◉	◉		772.0	«..Alamo..«	2072	4.02	d		
	9.01	◉		776.6	«..Java..«	2045	3.46	d		
	9.20	◉		784.6	«..Selby..«	1877	3.29	d		
	s9.34	◉		792.7	«..Sitka..«	1766	s3.10	d		
	9.45	◉		796.9	«..Glenham..«	1679	3.00	d		
10.33	10.05	10.55		805.7	Ar..Mobridge..Lv	1653	*2.40	*9.40		*1055
AM	AM	PM			Central Time		PM	PM		AM

a Stops to let off passengers from points west of Miles City destined to points on the Linton line.

b Stops to let off passengers from points west of Mobridge destined to points on the Fargo line.

c Will stop to let off passengers ticketed from points on Sou. Minn. Div.

d Will stop to let off passengers from the Moreau River, Cheyenne River and Standing Rock branches.

e Stops on signal for passengers for Mobridge and East.

f Stops on signal to take on passengers for Miles City and points west where No. 15 is scheduled to stop.

◉ Will stop to pick up passengers for points west of Miles City.

◆ Will stop to let off passengers from points west of Miles City.

+ Will stop to let off passengers from points east of Aberdeen.

▲ Will stop to let off passengers from points west of Miles City and to pick up passengers for Aberdeen and points beyond.

CHICAGO, MILWAUKEE & PUGET SOUND RY.

Chicago—Milwaukee—St. Paul—Minneapolis Aberdeen—Butte—Seattle—Tacoma—Continued. 8-19-12

Table 14 — Mountain Time

3	15	17	Mls.	C. M. & P. S. Ry.	Elevation	18	16	6
AM	PM	AM				PM	AM	PM
*1005	*1005	*9.45	805.7	Lv. Mobridge. Ar	1653	8.30	9.45	1.30
			810.4	Ar Moreau Jct «		▲		
10.32		+	817.6	«..Wakpala..«	1633	▲		1.02
10.53		+	828.4	«..Mahto..«	1805	▲		12.42
11.07	11.02	+	836.1	«..McLaughlin..«	1996	7.29		12.27
s1122		+	844.4	«..Cadillac..«	2160	▲		s1210
11.35		+	851.3	«..Walker..«	2162	▲		11.57
11.47		+	857.3	«..Tatanka..«	2204	▲		s1147
12.02	11.44	11.31	864.3	«..McIntosh..«	2270	6.35	7.50	11.21
12.31		+	874.1	«..Watauga..«	2248	▲		11.05
12.47		+	882.6	«..Morristown..«	2233	▲		10.50
12.57		+	887.2	«..Keldron..«	2250	▲		10.40
1.13		+	895.2	«..Thunder Hawk..«	2579	▲		10.23
1.31	12.51	12.47	904.5	«..Lemmon, S.D..«	2567	5.35	6.50	10.04
1 43		+	910.4	«..Petrel, N.D..«	2555	▲		9.53
2 01		+	920.1	«..Haynes..«	2540	▲		9.33
2.17	1.28	1 26	928.2	«..Hettinger..«	2668	4.55	6.13	9.17
2 38		+	936.6	«..Bucyrus..«	2775	▲		9.01
2.58		+	945.8	«..Reeder..«	2806	▲		8.45
3.12		+	952.1	«..Gascoyne..«	2754	▲		8.32
3.20		+	955.6	«..Scranton..«	2770	▲		8.27
3.31		+	960.4	«..Buffalo Springs..«	2850	5.17	5.05	8.17
3.47	2.34	2 35	968.1	«..Bowman..«	2958	3.47	5.05	8.06
4.05		+	975.4	«..Griffin..«	3045	▲		7.52
4.20		+	981.6	«..Rhame..«	3178	▲		7.40
4.30		+	986.3	«..Ives..«	3083	▲		s7.29
4.45		+	992.2	«..Berger..«	2800	▲		s7.16
5.00	3.19	3 25	995.6	«..Marmarth..«	2707	2.39	3.53	7.00
s5.25		+	1002.4	«Montline, N.D..«	2830	▲		s6.49
s5.35		+	1006.7	«..Dodge, Mont..«	2929	▲		s6.41
s5.45		+	1010.8	«..Kingmont..«	3020	▲		s6.33
6.00	f4.01	4.14	1016.8	«..Baker..«	2929	2.00	e3.09	6 23
s6.15		+	1023.0	«..Tonquin..«	2837	▲		s6.09
6.27		+	1028.7	«..Plevna..«	2750	▲		5.59
6.43		+	1036.4	«..Westmore..«	2643	▲		5.45
7.00		5.04	1044.5	«..Ismay..«	2519	1 07	e2.18	s5.18
s7.15		+	1051.3	«..Lacomb..«	2453	▲		5.03
7.32		5.29	1059.6	«..Mildred..«	2357	12.40		s4.45
s7.48		+	1067.4	«..Whitney..«	2274	▲		s4.45
s8.02		+	1074.0	«..Bluffport..«	2242	▲		4.30
8.18		6.08	1081.2	«..Terry..«	2243	12.03	e1.11	4.15
s8.30		+	1087.2	«..Calypso..«	2240	▲		s4.00
8.44		+	1093.5	«..Saugus..«	2251	▲		3.47
s8.57		+	1099.7	«..Bonfield..«	2273	▲		s3.34
9.10		+	1105.4	«..Kinsey..«	2307	▲		3.21
s9.25		+	1112.9	«..Tusler..«	2336	▲		s3.05
9.40	6.34	7.16	1120.0	«..Miles City..«	2354	10.39	11 54	*2.50
PM		s7.40	1128.2	«..Paragon..«	2404	s1025		AM
		s7.53	1135.6	«..Calabar..«	2415	s1011	◉	
		s8.10	1145.3	«..Thurlow..«	2462	s9.53	◉	
		s8.22	1152.5	«..Carterville..«	2487	s9.39	◉	
		s8.33	1159.4	«..Orinoco..«	2503	s9.26	◉	
	7.54	8.45	1164.6	«..Forsyth..«	2529	9.16	10.41	
		s8.50	1167.7	«..Malaga..«	2534	s9.06	◉	
		s9.05	1176.5	«..Antwerp..«	2599	s8.52	◉	
		s9.20	1182.0	«..Vananda..«	2699	s8.42	◉	
		s9.31	1187.3	«..Rahway..«	2876	s8.30	◉	
		s9.45	1192.2	«..Heritage..«	2876	s8.20	◉	
		*9.57	1197.4	«..Thebes..«	2914	s8.10	◉	
		s1012	1204.6	«..Ingomar..«	3035	s7.56	◉	
		s1025	1211.0	«..Galbraith..«	2968	s7.44	◉	
		s1036	1214.9	«..Sumatra..«	3181	s7.36	◉	
		s1046	1220.2	«..Hibbard..«	3066	s7.23	◉	
31		s1056	1225.4	«..Bascom..«	2930	s7.12	◉	**30**
AM		11.07						PM
*6.30	9.42	11.07	1231.7	«..Melstone..«	2897	6.55	8 32	8.10
s6.43		+	1237.2	«..Japan..«	2941	◉		s7.55
6.54		11.35	1243.2	«..Musselshell..«	2991	6.32	◉	7.44
7.08		+	1250.0	«..Delphia..«	3049	◉		7.32
7.24		+	1258.7	«..Gage..«	3123	◉		7.13
7.42	10.42	12.25	1266.1	«..Roundup..«	3184	5.49	7.39	6.57
8.00		+	1275.7	«..Elso..«	3269	◉		6.36
8.14		+	1282.8	«..Waldheim..«	3343	◉		6.22
8.31		+	1291.1	«..Lavina..«	3439	◉		6.06
s8.47		+	1299.1	«..Burgoyne..«	3532	◉		s5.51
9.03		+	1306.9	«..Ryegate..«	3638	◉		5.37
9.14		+	1313.1	«..Barber..«	3721	◉		5.25
9.28		+	1320.3	«..Shawmut..«	3857	◉		5.12
s9.44		+	1328.2	«..Pontiac.. Ar	4008	◉		s4.56
10.00	12.40	2.43	1336.3	Ar. Harlowton. Lv	4163	*3.35	*5.57	*4.40
AM	PM	AM				AM	PM	PM

Will stop to let off passengers from points east of Mobridge.

◉ Will stop to take on passengers for points east of Mobridge.

Continued on pages 27 and 28.

OLYMPIAN TIMETABLE of 1912.

Roy Jorgensen
The Milwaukee Road

Chicago, Milwaukee & St. Paul Ry.
CHICAGO, MILWAUKEE & PUGET SOUND RAILWAY.
Chicago—Milwaukee—St. Paul—Minneapolis
Aberdeen—Butte—Seattle—Tacoma—Continued. 8-11-12
Continued from pages 25 and 26.

33	15	17	Mls.	Table 15 Mountain Time.	Elevation	18	16	34
AM	PM	AM		C. M. & P. S. Ry.		AM	PM	PM
*1010	1250	*2.53	1336.3	Lv... Harlowton ...Ar	4163	3.25	5.47	2.25
10.38	#	#	1348.3	Ar... Two Dot ...«	4427	◉	◉	1.58
s1051	#	#	1354.7	«... Selkirk ...«	4623	◉	◉	s1.45
11.04	#	#	1360.6	«... Martinsdale ...«	4811	◉	◉	1.33
11.15	5.10	#	1365.0	«... Groveland ...«	4998	◉	◉	1.20
11.32	#	#	1372.0	«... Lennep ...«	5225	◉	◉	1.04
11.56	#	#	1381.9	«... Summit ...«	5788	◉	◉	12.44
12.26	2.34	#	1393.8	«... Ringling ...«	5288	◉	4.04	12.15
*1232	#	#	1397.3	«... Minden ...«	5209	◉	◉	s1204
12.46	#	#	1404.2	«... Sixteen ...«	4969	◉	◉	11.48
1.04	#	#	1412.1	«... Josephine ...«	4643	◉	◉	11.28
1.17	#	#	1416.1	«... Maudlow ...«	4455	◉	◉	11.13
s1.27	#	#	1424.0	«... Deer Park ...«	4206	◉	◉	s1102
s1.37	#	#	1428.6	«... Crane ...«	4041	◉	◉	s1052
1.43	3.50	6.11	1431.2	«... Lombard ...«	3987	12.12	2.24	10.47
s1.49	#	#	1434.3	«... Barron ...«	3971	◉	◉	s1039
s2.00	#	#	1442.1	«... Eustis ...«	4017	◉	◉	s1025
2.15	4.22	6.45	1450.6	«.. Three Forks ...«	4066	11.26	1.35	10.00
2.37	#	s7.07	1457.0	«... Willow Creek ...«	4145	s1114	◉	9.48
2.49	#	s7.18	1463.5	«... Sappington ...«	4185	s1101	◉	9.36
s2.59	#	s7.27	1468.4	«... Alcazar ...«	4232	s1051	◉	s9.26
3.12	#	s7.40	1475.1	« Jefferson Island «	4263	s1038	◉	9.13
3.30		8.00	1484.8	«... Piedmont ...«	4357	10.20	12.34	8.55
s3.48	#	s8.18	1490.5	«... Vendome ...«	4817	s1005	◉	s8.39
s4.00	#	s8.30	1494.2	«... Cedric ...«	5178	s9.57	◉	s8.30
4.17	#	s8.47	1499.8	«... Grace ...«	5664	s9.44	◉	8.15
4.41	#	s9.10	1505.7	«... Donald ...«	6322	s9.28	◉	7.58
s4.45	#	s9.14	1507.8	«... Penfield ...«	6246	s9.20	◉	s7.52
4.59	#	s9.27	1512.5	«... Janney ...«	5869	s9.07	◉	s7.36
s5.08	#	s9.35	1516.1	«... Newcomb ...«	5617	s8.58	◉	s7.24
5.30	7.15	9.57	1523.8	«... Butte ...«	5538	8.30	10.43	*7.00
PM								AM
	#	s1053	1548.0	«... Morel ...«	4870	s7.38	◉	
	#	s1105	1556.3	«... Sinclair ...«	4675	s7.22	◉	
	8.40	11.15	1564.1	«... Deer Lodge ...«	4520	6 57	9.15	
	#	s1143	1575.5	«... Garrison ...«	4315	s6.33	◉	
	#	s1156	1582.8	«... Gold Creek ...«	4190	s6.15	◉	
	#	12.16	1595.0	«... Drummond ...«	3945	5.55	8.22	
	#	s1233	1605.6	«... Bearmouth ...«	3800	s5.39	◉	
	#	s1250	1615.4	«... Ravenna ...«	3665	s5.24	◉	
	#	1.10	1626.9	«... Clinton ...«	3450	s5.04	◉	
	11.00	1.40	1643.4	«... Missoula ...«	3190	4.38	7.05	
	#	1.58	1653.0	«... Primrose ...«	3070	4.17	◉	
	#	s2.07	1659.5	«... Frenchtown ...«	3025	s4.09	◉	
	#	s2.15	1664.4	«... Huson ...«	3015	s4.01	◉	
	11.59	2.35	1675.0	«... Alberton ...«	3040	3.34	5.55	
	#	3.48	1706.1	«... Superior ...«	2720	2.42	5 07	
	s4.51	5.00	1718.2	«... St. Regis ...«	2680	2.19	◉	
		5.00	1787.5	«... Haugan ...«	3150	1.34	◉	
	s6.30		1768.0	«... Falcon ...«	3390	12.10	◉	
4.25	7.15		1775.4	Ar } Avery { Lv	2495	11.34	2.05	
3.35	6.25			Lv } { Ar	2495	10.24	12.55	
4.52	7.45		1818.1	Ar... St. Joe ...« Pacific Time	2140	9.10	11.38	
5.20	8 15		1824.9	«... St. Maries ...«	2145	8.45	11.13	
	#	9.15	1831.2	«... Ramsdell ...«	2145	s8.28	◉	
	#	9.15	1845.2	«... Plummer ...«	2725	7.55	10.24	
	s9.25		1848.4	«... Sorrento ...«	2800	s7.45	◉	
	6.52	9 53	1859.4	«... Tekoa, Wash ...«	2590	7.25	9 53	
	s1022		1872.8	«... Pandora ...«	2395	s6.55	◉	
	7.45	10 37	1879.5	«... Rosalia ...«	2240	6.41	9 14	
	8.10	11.00	1888.8	«... Malden ...«	2070	6.13	8.45	
	#	11.17	1891.6	«... Pine City ...«	2015	6.04	◉	
	#	s1146	1905.0	«... Lavista ...«	1805	s5.35	◉	
	#	s1220	1917.7	«... Revere ...«	1600	s5.11	◉	
	#	s1247	1930.6	«... Marengo ...«	1675	s4.48	◉	
	#	1.10	1942.1	«... Ralston ...«	1650	4.28	◉	
	10.35	1.38	1956.2	«... Lind ...«	1405	4.02	6.44	
	#	s2.03	1969.2	«... Roxboro ...«	1245	s3.37	◉	
	11.20	2.22	1971.1	«... Warden ...«	1275	3.19	6 05	
	11.45	2.48	1991.9	«... Othello ...«	1050	2.48	5 30	
	s3.16		2000.9	«... Taunton ...«	870	2.30	◉	
	s1222	3.27	2006.3	«... Corfu ...«	760	2.21	s5.05	
	#	s3.40	2012.8	«... Colletta ...«	640	2.10	◉	
	#	s3.47	2016.5	«... Smyrna ...«	555	2.02	◉	
	#	4.15	2028.1	«... Beverly ...«	545	1.41	4 30	
	#	s4.50	2039.9	«... Rye ...«	1720	1.07	◉	
45	1 05							**46**
PM	2.12	5.15	2047.7	«... Boylston ...«	2390	12.43	3 31	PM
*1.40	2.36	5.45	2056.8	«... Kittitas ...«	1645	12.14	3.02	12.55
1 52	2 50	6.00	2062.9	«... Ellensburg ...«	1590	12.01	2.50	12.43
2 05	#	6.20	2070.4	«... Thorp ...«	1655	s1147	◉	12.30
2.20	#	s6.38	2078.3	«... Horlick ...«	1780	s1130	◉	12.15
2.40	3.47	6.58	2088.1	Ar... Cle-Elum ...Lv	1945	*1110	*2.03	*1155
PM	PM	AM				P.M	PM	AM

Chicago, Milwaukee & St. Paul Ry.
CHICAGO, MILWAUKEE & PUGET SOUND RAILWAY.
Chicago—Milwaukee—St. Paul—Minneapolis
Aberdeen—Butte—Seattle—Tacoma—Continued. 6-16-12

45	15	17	Mls.	Table 16 Pacific Time.	Elevation	18	16	46
PM	PM	AM		C. M. & P. S. Ry.		PM	PM	AM
*2.50	*3.57	*7.08	2088.1	Lv... Cle-Elum ...Ar	1945	11.00	1.53	11.45
s3.09	#	#	2095.7	Ar... Lavender ...«	2110	◉	◉	s1128
3.18	#	s 7.33	2099.9	«... Easton ...«	2180	10.36	◉	11.18
3.38	#	#	2108.4	«... Whittier ...«	2450	◉	◉	s1100
3.53	#	8.05	2115.0	«... Keechelus ...«	2560	◉	◉	10.45
4.10	5.10	8.20	2119.7	«... Laconia ...«	3010	9.58	12.50	10.29
4.25	#	s 8.33	2124.1	«... Rockdale ...«	2480	◉	◉	10.12
s4.40	#	s 8.47	2128.5	«... Bandera ...«	2120	◉	◉	s9.57
5.00	#	s 9.06	2134.4	«... Garcia ...«	1625	◉	◉	9.38
s5.17	#	s 9.22	2139.6	«... Ragnar ...«	1190	◉	◉	s9.22
5.30	6.20	9.30	2143.1	«.. Cedar Falls ...«	930	8.42	11.42	9.10
5.56	#	#	2156.4	«... Landsberg ...«	636	◉	◉	8.43
6.10	7.03	10.11	2160.0	«.. Maple Valley ...«	295	8.07	◉	8.30
s6.21	#	#	2163.8	«.. Cedar Mountain..«	195	◉	◉	s8.19
s6.28	#	#	2166.8	«... Elliott ...«	120	◉	◉	s8.13
6.37	s7.27	g10.41	2170.3	«... Renton ...«	25	g7.41	g1041	8.02
s6.46 **101**			2172.9	«... Black River ...«	20		s7.56	**102**
			2177.0	«... Van Asselt ...«	15			
AM			2179.0	«... Argo ...«	15			s7.47 PM
*720	7.10	8.00	11.10	2182.5	«... Seattle ...Lv	15	7.15	10.15	*7.35
s752 PM	s8 47	g11.55	2179.2	«... Kent ...Ar	65	◉	◉	AM s1.29
s802	s9.00	g12.04	2185.0	«... Auburn ...«	105	◉	◉	s1 20
s814	s9.10	g12.14	2191.8	«... Sumner ...«	0	◉	◉	s1.08
s818	#	g12.18	2193.8	«... No. Puyallup ...«	70	◉	◉	s1.04
8.35 AM	9.30	12.35	2201.2	Ar... Tacoma ...Lv	80	*5.45 PM	*8.45 AM	*1245 PM

For explanation of # and ◉ see page 26.
g Train stops on signal for passengers to and from Ellensburg and points east.
Additional Chicago, Milwaukee & Puget Sound train schedules on pages 78, 79 and 80.

Equipment—Chicago, St. Paul, Minneapolis, Tacoma and Seattle

No. 1-101, **The Pioneer Limited, Electric Lighted**—(Minneapolis Section)—Compartment car, standard sleeping cars, observation-buffet car and coaches Chicago to St. Paul-Minneapolis. Standard sleeping car Milwaukee to La Crosse. Parlor car and dining car Chicago to Milwaukee.

No. 1-101, **The Pioneer Limited, Electric Lighted**—(St. Paul Section)—Compartment car, standard sleeping cars, library-buffet car and coaches Chicago to St. Paul-Minneapolis. Standard sleeping car Chicago to New Lisbon and Milwaukee to New Lisbon (for Wis. Val. Div.). Standard sleeping car Milwaukee to St. Paul-Minneapolis. Dining car Chicago to Milwaukee.

No. 4, **The Pioneer Limited—Electric Lighted**—Compartment and standard sleeping cars, library-buffet car and coaches Minneapolis-St. Paul to Chicago. Standard sleeping car Minneapolis-St. Paul to Milwaukee. Parlor car and dining car Milwaukee to Chicago.

No. 2, **Electric Lighted**—Coaches Minneapolis-St. Paul to Milwaukee, and Milwaukee to Chicago. Standard sleeping car La Crosse to Milwaukee. Standard sleeping car New Lisbon to Milwaukee (from Minocqua), and New Lisbon to Milwaukee (from Star Lake). Standard sleeping car and coach Milwaukee to Chicago (from Calumet via D. S. S. & A. Ry.). Standard sleeping car Milwaukee to Chicago (from Marquette via D. S. S. & A. Ry.). Calumet and Marquette equipment into Milwaukee on Superior Div. No. 2.

No. 3, **Electric Lighted**—See "Equipment" pages 31 and 62.

No. 5, **Electric Lighted**—Observation-parlor cars and coaches between Chicago and St. Paul-Minneapolis. Dining car Milwaukee to St. Paul-Minneapolis.

No. 6, **Electric Lighted**—Observation-parlor cars, dining car and coaches Minneapolis-St. Paul to Chicago.

Nos. 15 and 16, **"The Olympian"—Electric Lighted**—Observation cars with library, smoking room, buffet, barber shop and bath, drawing-room-compartment and standard sleeping cars, tourist sleeping cars, dining cars and coaches between Chicago and Seattle and Tacoma. Standard sleeping cars between Chicago and Minneapolis.

Nos. 17 and 18, **"The Columbian"—Electric Lighted—Drawing-room** and standard sleeping cars, tourist sleeping cars, dining cars and coaches between Chicago and Seattle and Tacoma. Standard sleeping car between St. Paul and Aberdeen (car open at 9.30 p.m.). Parlor cars between Chicago and Minneapolis.

Nos. 22 and 25, **Electric Lighted**—See "Equipment" pages 31 and 62.

No. 55, **Fast Mail**—Coaches Milwaukee to St. Paul-Minneapolis. Cafe observation car La Crosse to Minneapolis.

No. 56, **The Fast Mail—Electric Lighted**—Compartment car, standard sleeping cars and coaches Minneapolis-St. Paul to Chicago. Cafe observation car Minneapolis-St. Paul to La Crosse.

H. & D. Division

Nos. 1 and 4—Coaches between St. Paul-Minneapolis and Aberdeen.
Nos. 3 and 6, **Electric Lighted**—Standard sleeping car between St. Paul-Minneapolis and Aberdeen. Coaches between St. Paul-Minneapolis and Miles City. Through standard sleeping car and coaches between St. Paul and Fargo. Dining car between St. Paul and Glencoe.